Return to an Order of the Honourable the
House of Commons dated March 2001 for the

Review of the Circumstances Surrounding an Application for Naturalisation by Mr S P Hinduja in 1998

Sir Anthony Hammond KCB, QC

Ordered by The House of Commons *to be printed*
9th March 2001

C 287   LONDON: THE STATIONERY OFFICE   £14

To the Prime Minister

The Right Honourable Tony Blair MP

CHAPTER 1

INTRODUCTION

1.1. On 24 January 2001, you asked me to carry out a Review with the following terms of reference:—

> "To establish what approaches were made to the Home Office in 1998 in connection with the possibility of an application for naturalisation by Mr S P Hinduja, and the full circumstances surrounding such approaches and the later grant of that application, and to report to you.".

In your answer to an oral question on 24 January 2001, you said that my findings would be published.

1.2. I started work on 25 January 2001 and, after an initial reading of the papers to which I then had access, it became clear that, in order for me to carry out a thorough investigation of the circumstances surrounding the application for naturalisation by Mr S P Hinduja, it was appropriate for me to look at the circumstances of the granting of naturalisation to Mr G P Hinduja because the circumstances of both applications were closely related. For the same reason, I decided that it was appropriate for me to look at the circumstances surrounding the enquiries about naturalisation in respect of Mr Prakash Hinduja. This was agreed by the Government and the Home Secretary announced it in a Written Answer to a Parliamentary Question from the Right Honourable Miss Ann Widdecombe MP on 30 January 2001. A copy of the Hansard Report of this Reply is attached at Annex A to this Report.

1.3. At this stage I need only say by way of further background to my Review that it was set up following the resignation of the Right Honourable Peter Mandelson MP, from his post as Secretary of State for Northern Ireland and this in turn had followed statements in the Press concerning his role in making enquiries in the summer of 1998 on behalf of Mr S P Hinduja, who was interested in obtaining naturalisation as a British citizen. I describe these events in more detail in subsequent Chapters of this Report.

1.4. From the outset, it was made clear to me that I would receive the complete co-operation of Government Ministers, Departments and officials and that I would have access to any information which I needed to carry out my terms of reference. This proved to be the case. Indeed no-one, whether within or outside Government, declined to be interviewed and all those whom I invited to interview co-operated fully in answering the questions which I put to them. Others volunteered information without an approach from me. I deal separately (Chapter 5) with the material held by the Security and Intelligence Services. A list of the Departments and individuals, whom I saw or from whom I sought information, is contained in Annex B.

1.5. A number of questions have been raised either directly with me or in the Press about the scope of my terms of reference and it may be helpful here for me to explain their scope, as I have interpreted them, both as regards those matters which I regard as appropriate for my Review to address and those which it is not.

1.6. It became clear to me that I could not deal satisfactorily with the events in the summer of 1998 and, in particular, the nature of the contacts between Mr Mandelson's office and that of Mr Mike O'Brien MP, the Home Office Minister in charge of Immigration and Naturalisation matters, at the time, without, also, looking at the events of December 2000 and January 2001, when it became necessary to examine those contacts in the context of a Parliamentary Question from Mr Norman Baker MP. To the extent to which it is necessary to give an account of what happened in 1998, I include an account of the events of December 2000 and January 2001. But, except for the purpose which I have described, it is no part of my function to examine the reasons which led to Mr Mandelson's resignation.

1.7. Secondly, I am not concerned with issues related to the sponsorship of the Dome, as such. I have, however, examined papers relating to the Dome in the Cabinet Office and the Department of Culture, Media and Sport, as well as the official papers covering Mr Mandelson's time as Secretary of State for Trade and Industry when he was also responsible for the Dome, to ascertain whether there was any evidence of any link between the naturalisation applications of the Hindujas and their sponsorship of the Dome. I deal with this issue in Chapter 8.

1.8. Thirdly, I do not regard it as within my terms of reference to investigate or comment on dealings or social contacts between Ministers or officials and the Hinduja brothers, except so far as is necessary to consider these matters in the context of the handling of their naturalisation applications.

1.9. Fourthly, I do not regard it as appropriate for me to express views on the application of the Ministerial Code of Conduct to the conduct of the Ministers whose actions were the subject of my Review, or on issues relating to the content of the Code. These are matters for others and there is well-established machinery for examining these issues, including the propriety of Ministers' actions as Members of Parliament.

1.10. In Chapter 5 of this Report I describe the part played by Mr Peter Mandelson in the events surrounding the second application for naturalisation by Mr S P Hinduja. Mr Mandelson was also involved in passing on an enquiry concerning Mr Prakash Hinduja (see Chapter 6). Mr Mandelson was represented, during my Review, by Goldsmiths, Solicitors and by Mr Jonathan Caplan QC. Both Mr Caplan and Mr Lee Goldsmith accompanied Mr Mandelson when I interviewed him. During that interview Mr Caplan made an important submission on the approach which I should adopt to issues of fact which are in dispute. In particular, he drew my attention to what was said by the late Lord Denning in his Report into the Profumo affair in 1963 (Cmnd 2152). In paragraph 7 of his Report, Lord Denning pointed out that his Inquiry was not a suitable body to determine guilt or innocence and witnesses had not given evidence on oath and could not be cross examined. In other words none of the safeguards available in a court of law were available. On the other hand, if he did not inquire into the matters which had been raised his Inquiry would not arrive at the truth. Mr Caplan urged me to adopt the same approach to questions of fact as that adopted by Lord Denning. In paragraph 8, Lord Denning said:—

> "When the facts are clear beyond controversy, I will state them as objectively as I can, irrespective of the consequences to individuals: and I will draw any inference that is manifest from those facts. But when the facts are in issue, I must always remember the cardinal principle of justice—that no man is to be condemned on suspicion. There must be evidence which proves his guilt before he is pronounced to be so. I will therefore take the facts in his favour rather than do an injustice which is without remedy. For from my findings there is no appeal.".

1.11. Mr Caplan also submitted that I should have regard to the reliability and quality of the evidence before me. I have given careful consideration to Mr Caplan's submissions. I should say immediately that the facts which I was asked to inquire into for the purposes of my Review are far removed from the scandalous events which were the subject of Lord Denning's Inquiry. Important issues of national security were at stake then. No such issues are involved in my Review. Nevertheless, the form of Review which I have been asked to undertake shares some features with those of Lord Denning's Inquiry. The reputations of individuals depend, to some extent, on the conclusions which I have been called upon to reach, although not to the extent of involving questions of criminal conduct, as did the Profumo affair. One Minister resigned as a result of the events which are the subject of my Review. My Review, also, has not had the advantage of some of the safeguards applicable in a court of law. The informality of the procedures which I have necessarily had to adopt carries with it both advantages and disadvantages, which, again, are discussed in paragraph 5 of Lord Denning's Report. I am also, of course, mindful of the criticisms of this form of Inquiry in and of the Recommendations of the Royal Commission on Tribunals of Inquiry, 1966, chaired by the late Lord Salmon (Cmnd. 3121).

1.12. I have come to the conclusion that I should adopt, broadly, the same approach as Lord Denning described in the passage quoted in paragraph 1.10 above. I have, of course, also had regard to the reliability and quality of the evidence presented to me, as suggested by Mr Caplan. In particular, I have considered whether it is first hand or not, whether it is consistent with other accounts of the same events and whether it is corroborated or capable of independent verification. I have also had regard to the fact that, in the case of events which occurred in 1998, i.e. more than two and a half years ago, recollections are hazy and it would not be surprising if accounts of different individuals are not wholly consistent with each other.

1.13. In view of the informality of the procedures which I adopted in carrying out my Review, and of the dangers which I have discussed in seeking to arrive at conclusions which affect the reputation of individuals, I have sought to proceed in a way which was designed both to be fair to those individuals and to ascertain, as far as possible, the truth of the events which I have reviewed. Individuals who gave evidence were given the opportunity to consider their role; to check, where necessary, their account of events with those of others who were involved in those events; and to comment on drafts of those parts of the Report which relate to the role which they played.

1.14. I have not interviewed any of the Hinduja brothers. There were obvious practical difficulties in visiting them in India, if my Review was to be completed within a reasonable timescale. But, more importantly, I have not found it necessary to do so. Their position is well known from their public statements, that is to say that they had done nothing wrong and, in particular, that at no time had they sought to link their attempts to obtain citizenship with their sponsorship of the Dome. I have come to the conclusion that interviewing them would have added nothing to the information which I have been able to obtain from other sources.

1.15. In the following Chapters of this Report I include a summary of my conclusions (Chapter 2). I deal, in turn, with the criteria which govern the consideration of applications for naturalisation as a British citizen and certain policy developments (Chapter 3), the case of Mr G P Hinduja (Chapter 4), the case of Mr S P Hinduja (Chapter 5) and the case of Mr Prakash Hinduja (Chapter 6). Chapter 7 concerns Mr Keith Vaz MP; Chapter 8 deals with the sponsorship of the Dome; and in Chapter 9 I offer some general conclusions on the methods of working in the private offices who were involved in the events described in my Report.

1.16. I have been assisted in carrying out my Review by Mr Tyson Hepple, who was appointed as the Secretary to the Review. I am greatly indebted to his expertise, skill and experience, which have been invaluable. He has worked assiduously and tirelessly to help me to complete my Review within the timetable which I set myself. I offer here my thanks and my appreciation for his work. I would also like to express my deep appreciation of the work of Mrs Denise Cramer, who acted as my Personal Assistant during the Review. Again, she worked tirelessly, against tight deadlines, to help me complete the Review and managed my office with skill and great good humour. She was ably assisted by Miss Sue Selva, to whom I am also very grateful. I should also like to thank others whom I do not name, who, at various stages, helped me in the preparation of my Report.

CHAPTER 2

SUMMARY OF CONCLUSIONS

My main conclusions are as follows.

2.1. The applications for naturalisation of Mr G P Hinduja and Mr S P Hinduja were handled properly and within established criteria. Certain aspects of the latter case should have been pursued more vigorously (Chapters 4 and 5).

2.2. No improper pressure was brought to bear by any Minister in respect of these applications (Chapters 4 and 5).

2.3. The enquiries made on behalf of Mr Prakash Hinduja were handled properly by all concerned (Chapter 6).

2.4. Mr Keith Vaz made representations on behalf of both Mr S P and Mr G P Hinduja, but these were in the context of many other immigration and nationality cases in which he made representations. There is no evidence of any improper relationship between him and the brothers (Chapter 7).

2.5. Mr Mandelson or his officials made or passed on enquiries to the Home Office on behalf of Mr S P Hinduja and Mr Prakash Hinduja. It is not possible to reach firm conclusions about the exact circumstances in which the contacts took place in relation to Mr S P Hinduja, but it is likely that Mr Mandelson spoke directly to Mr O'Brien. Mr Mandelson's belief that he had not had a telephone conversation with Mr O'Brien was honestly held. Mr Mandelson did not make representations on behalf of either Mr S P or Mr Prakash Hinduja. There is no evidence of any improper relationship between him and the Hindujas or of any connection between his contacts between them over the sponsorship of the Dome and their efforts to obtain naturalisation (Chapters 5, 6 and 8).

2.6. There was intelligence material about the Hinduja brothers, but this was not drawn to the attention of the Home Office and it, probably, would not have affected the outcome of the naturalisation applications if it had been (Chapter 5).

2.7. In some respects, the processing of the naturalisation applications by the Home Office could have been improved, but systems are now in place which address these issues (Chapter 5).

2.8. Record keeping in the private offices involved in the matters under Review was, in some respects, unsatisfactory and there is a need to address this issue and that of the monitoring of telephone calls (Chapter 9).

CHAPTER 3

RELEVANT LAW AND PRACTICE RELATING TO NATURALISATION

3.1. The requirements which have to be satisfied before a person may be granted naturalisation as a British citizen are contained in section 6 of and Schedule 1 to the British Nationality Act 1981. My Review is concerned only with section 6(1) of the Act (section 6(2) is concerned with applications based on marriage to a British citizen and is not relevant to the events described in the Report). Section 6 and Schedule 1 are set out in full in Annex C .

3.2. The important features of these requirements, for the purposes of my Review, are:—

(a) that the applicant is of good character;

(b) that his intention is to make his principal home in the United Kingdom;

(c) that he was in the United Kingdom at the beginning of the period of five years ending with the date of the application;

(d) that the number of days in which he was absent from the United Kingdom during that period did not exceed 450; and

(e) that the number of days in which he was so absent in the final twelve months period did not exceed 90.

A significant point is that the Secretary of State may, if he thinks fit "in the special circumstances of any particular case", relax the requirements in (d) and (e) above so as to accept longer periods of absence than the periods of 450 and 90 days respectively specified in those sub paragraphs.

On the other hand, it is necessary to stress that what cannot be waived is the requirement that a person should be "in" the United Kingdom at the beginning of the five year period.

3.3. An important change of approach to the question of absences of applicants during the five year period is signalled in a letter sent by Mr Andrew Walmsley in the Home Office Nationality Directorate to a firm of solicitors dated 14 April 1998. Because of the lifting of embarkation controls after which it became less easy to calculate the exact period of absences from the stamps in passports, the letter says that guidance to staff emphasised the need to look at an applicant's overall position in the country rather than to become bogged down in the mechanical process of establishing the exact number of days' absence.

3.4. One of the issues which has attracted public comment in connection with the way in which the cases of the Hindujas were handled is in what circumstances the Home Office was prepared to give priority to a particular application rather than to let it take its place in the queue. This is against the position that the average time to complete the processing of a naturalisation application under section 6(1) of the 1981 Act is currently just over 14 months. In February 1990, when the Hindujas submitted their first applications, the waiting time for a section 6(1) application was 27 months. In March 1997, when Mr G P Hinduja submitted his second application, the waiting time was 15.4 months. In October 1998, when Mr S P Hinduja submitted his second application, the waiting time was 20.1 months, although the waiting time has been gradually decreasing. A list of the criteria which the Home Office apply for the granting of priority is attached at Annex D. A relevant issue for the handling of the Hindujas' cases is the first of the listed criteria, i.e. that the applicant needs to travel urgently and is unable, or finds it difficult, to travel on his existing passport. In addition, it seems clear that where a second application from the same person is being considered, priority may be granted, because much of the necessary information required to check an application will often have been obtained when the first application was considered. A further point worth noting is that the Home Office, with the approval of Ministers, took the view during the period with which my Review is concerned that, if representations were made about a case which necessitated inspecting the papers in order to deal with the representations, it was often sensible to deal with the application itself rather than to return the papers to the queue to be dealt with in the normal way.

3.5. In July 1998, a White Paper entitled "Fairer, Faster and Firmer—A Modern Approach to Immigration and Asylum" (Cmnd 4018) was published. The only part of the White Paper which is relevant to this Review is Chapter 10, entitled "Encouraging Citizenship". Paragraph 10.2 refers to the fact that there was little positive encouragement to encourage people who want to do so, to become British. It then states:

> "The Government believes that more should be done to promote citizenship positively amongst the immigrant population, reflecting the multi-cultural and multi-racial society which we have become.".

The chapter goes on to discuss ways of quickening up the process of granting naturalisation. Finally, paragraph 10.7 discusses the Government's desire to create a more flexible approach to the residence requirements in the British Nationality Act 1981, pointing out that many of those who travel abroad on behalf of firms in this country, and who contribute to the economic well-being of the country, cannot satisfy the present residence requirements. (A copy of Chapter 10 of the White Paper is attached at Annex E). There is further discussion of this part of the consideration of the handling of Mr S P Hinduja's second application for naturalisation in Chapter 5.

CHAPTER 4

G P HINDUJA

The Hinduja Brothers

4.1. There are four brothers named Hinduja; these include Gopichand (known as "GP"), Srichand (known as "SP") and Prakash (known as "PP"). They are wealthy international businessmen with extensive interests in India and in other countries including the United Kingdom. I have already explained in Chapter 1 of this Report why I have concluded that I should review not only the circumstances relating to the application for naturalisation in 1998 of Mr S P Hinduja, but also those relating to the grant of naturalisation to Mr G P Hinduja and the enquiries made in 2000 on behalf of Mr Prakash Hinduja. Although it is unnecessary for me to go into earlier applications by the Hindujas in great detail, it is easier to put the later applications in context if I give an outline of what happened on the earlier occasion.

History from 1990-1996—the first application

4.2. An initial application was received from Mr G P Hinduja on 21 February 1990 supported by Sir Shapoor Reporter and Sir Jay Gohel, as referees. These were apparently sent to the then Home Secretary, the Right Honourable Kenneth Baker MP, and forwarded to the Nationality Department for processing in the normal way. The application seems to have been given priority because of the substantial enquiries which would be required before it could be determined. A more detailed discussion on the application of the priority criteria is contained in Chapter 5 in relation to Mr S P Hinduja. Mr G P Hinduja had entered the United Kingdom in 1982 and had obtained indefinite leave to remain here on 18 July 1985. The normal checks were made with the police and Security Service, which were negative (i.e. no adverse comments). In view of the fact that investigations were being carried out in India into alleged corruption relating to the award of an army contract to the Swedish firm Bofors, enquiries were made of the Foreign and Commonwealth Office and the Security Service was contacted again. The Security Service response was again negative. The FCO suggested that his application should be treated in the same way as any other application; as long as he remained under suspicion and investigation in India, it would cause considerable difficulty with the Indian Government if his application was given special treatment.

4.3. On 25 March 1991 a submission was put forward by Mr Doug McQueen recommending refusal of his application on the grounds, first, that he appeared not to meet the unwaivable requirements of being "in" the United Kingdom on the date on which the five year application period began; and secondly, on the basis that, because of the Bofors allegations, it would be difficult to satisfy the requirement of being of "good character." There was also some doubt about whether he had genuinely "thrown in his lot" with the United Kingdom. Mr Hinduja was told by the Nationality Department only that his application was refused on the grounds of his failure to comply with the residence requirements. This was not standard practice at the time although, in this case, Ministers agreed that the Hindujas should be told that they did not fulfil the residence requirements, but not that there were also doubts about the "good character" requirement. A copy of the submission and the note confirming that Ministers were content are attached at Annex F. On 3 April 1991, the Home Secretary decided that the application should be refused. I am satisfied that this application was dealt with properly and in accordance with the Nationality rules.

4.4. Between 1993 and 1996 enquiries about progress or representations were made on behalf of the Hindujas by a number of people including the Right Honourable Edward Heath MP, Sir Jay Gohel, Mr Keith Vaz MP, The Right Honourable Dame Angela Rumbold MP and Lord Feldman. It is only necessary to observe in relation to the last mentioned that he was told in a letter dated 1 July 1996 by the then Home Secretary, The Rt Honourable Michael Howard MP, (in accordance with the advice of Mr McQueen) that, unless the brothers had reduced the extent of their absences from the United Kingdom, any re-application would be unlikely to be successful. He was also told that the then Parliamentary Under Secretary of State, Mr Timothy Kirkhope MP, would be happy to discuss it with him. He was also informed in the same letter that Mr Walmsley in the Nationality Directorate (as it was now called) would be able to advise them on their chances of success if they could give an indication of their current level of absences. Another enquiry from Lord Feldman in October 1996 seems to have received a similar response, although there is no copy of any letter on the file.

History from March 1997-November 1997—the second application

4.5. On 3 March 1997 a second application for naturalisation was received from Mr G P Hinduja supported by Lord Feldman and the Right Honourable Sir Edward Heath, MP, as referees. A letter was sent by Mr Walmsley to Mr Vaz informing him of the re-application. This was in response to a letter of 24 February 1997 from Mr Vaz, which is not on the file. I have obtained a copy of it from Mr Vaz himself and it simply enquires about progress on the applications from Mr G P and Mr S P Hinduja. It seems that Mr Walmsley decided that in view of the high profile of the Hinduja brothers and of the political sensitivities of any application from them, it would be better to wait until after the election before going to Ministers about making a decision.

4.6. On 3 July 1997, Mr Walmsley put forward a submission to Mr O'Brien recommending that Mr Hinduja's current application for naturalisation should be granted. A copy of this submission is attached at Annex G. It was cleared with Mr A R Rawsthorne, Mr Walmsley's superior, in draft. Mr Rawsthorne made a few minor amendments, but otherwise agreed. This submission recited the history of the earlier application and rehearsed the reasons why the application should now be granted. The absences of Mr Hinduja amounted to 540 days compared to the 450 requirement in Schedule 1 to the 1981 Act (which can be relaxed—see Chapter 3 above). The submission stated that in deciding whether to relax this requirement in favour of an applicant, the Home Office would normally take into account whether he had established his home and family in the United Kingdom, whether he had transferred the bulk of his estate to the United Kingdom and the reasons for his absences. In Mr Hinduja's case, he had been resident here for 15 years. His wife and adult children lived here and were applying for citizenship separately; his company, Sangan Ltd, was established here (although the centre of the brothers' business empire remained in India) and his absences were caused primarily by business trips abroad. In view of these factors, Mr Walmsley recommended that the "excess" absences be waived.

4.7. Mr Walmsley went on to deal with the "good character" requirement, both because the Inland Revenue was said to be investigating the affairs of the Hinduja brothers and because of the Bofors affair, which had been mentioned at the time of the previous application. The Inland Revenue had confirmed that Mr Hinduja's tax affairs were up-to-date and in good order. As regards the Bofors affair, in November 1996, Mr Walmsley, following one of Lord Feldman's enquiries, again consulted the South Asian Department of the FCO about the Bofors investigation and the assessment of the effect on bilateral relations with India of a decision either to grant or refuse an application. He also enquired about the extent of the Hindujas' alleged involvement in the Bofors' affair. Ms Caroline Elmes, the Head of the South Asian Department, had replied, stating that the Hinduja family were controversial figures and that rumours of their involvement persisted. It was "conceivable" that the case could come alight. In conclusion, however, she said that the FCO did not believe that the Indian Government would be particularly concerned by a decision either to grant or refuse Mr G P Hinduja British nationality. Before replying to the Home Office, the British High Commission to India had been consulted over the reply. The High Commission made some drafting amendments to the draft reply. They said that making the Hindujas British citizens could still become an embarrassment to HMG and recommended that the draft should maintain its clearly unenthusiastic tone. The amendments were incorporated in the reply. It should be noted that it did not recommend that the Home Office should refuse naturalisation. The FCO were only asked for their views of the effect on bilateral relations with India if naturalisation were either granted or refused. A copy of Ms Elmes' letter is attached at Annex H. Mr Walmsley said in his submission that, although the Bofors affair was not dead, interest in it had lessened, the Indian Authorities would be unlikely to be concerned one way or another, and after such a length of time without any proceedings being initiated against Mr Hinduja, it would not seem right to continue to harbour doubts about his ability to meet the "good character" requirement. Mr Walmsley had not checked again with the FCO before submitting his minute of 3 July 1997. I can understand why he did not do that, but had he done so, he would have discovered that in fact there had been a major and (in India) well-publicised development in the Bofors investigation in January 1997 when the Indian authorities had received important information from the Swiss authorities which they had been seeking since 1990.

4.8. There is no record on the Nationality Directorate's file of any response to this submission, but Mr O'Brien confirmed that he accepted the recommendation. In an interview with me, Mr Walmsley has confirmed that his recommendation to grant naturalisation was accepted and naturalisation was granted to Mr Hinduja in November 1997.

Conclusions on the Handling of These Applications

4.9. The first application of Mr G P Hinduja appears to have been handled properly by all concerned, Ministers and officials. (I discuss the application of the criteria for prioritising applications in more detail in Chapter 5.) The second application was also, in my view, handled properly by officials and Ministers. The only issue which I think calls for comment is whether it was right to conclude that the "good character" requirement was satisfied, in view of the Bofors scandal and of the somewhat unenthusiastic terms of Ms Caroline Elmes' letter in November 1996, and whether Mr Walmsley should have consulted the FCO again, in view of the time which had elapsed since her letter. There was a case for consulting the FCO again, but Mr Walmsley had not noticed any renewal of interest in the Bofors scandal. I do not think that he should be criticised on that score. Whether the application should have been refused on the basis that the scandal cast doubt on whether Mr Hinduja satisfied the "good character" requirement is a matter of judgment. It will be recalled that this was an additional reason for refusing the earlier application in April 1991. The Swiss development was new, but it seems doubtful if it would have made a crucial difference to the outcome. It seems to me that, in all the circumstances, it was a reasonable judgment by officials that the application should not be refused on that ground. Mr O'Brien was perfectly entitled to accept Mr Walmsley's advice and I do not think that his judgment can be faulted.

CHAPTER 5

S P HINDUJA

5.1. The second application for citizenship by Mr Srichand (S P) Hinduja in 1998 is at the centre of my terms of reference and turned out to be the most significant part of my Review.

5.2. Mr S P Hinduja is the eldest brother. He came to the United Kingdom in 1981 and was granted Indefinite Leave to Remain in 1985.

SP Hinduja's first application for citizenship

5.3. Mr S P Hinduja first applied for naturalisation on 21 February 1990. His referees on this application were Sir Shapoor Reporter and Sir Jay Gohel. The application form and supporting documentation were sent directly to the Home Secretary's office. The application was sent on to the Nationality Department on 22 March 1990.

5.4. On 30 April 1990 Mr S P Hinduja passed a letter to the then Prime Minister, Mrs Thatcher, at a reception, which was, in turn, sent to the Home Office for attention. The letter enquired about whether progress was being made in respect of the application for naturalisation. On 15 May 1990, the Home Secretary's private secretary wrote to the Prime Minister's private secretary advising him that consideration of the application would now begin.

5.5. It seems that , as in the case of Mr G P Hinduja (Chapter 4 above), priority was given to the case on the basis that a significant number of enquiries would need to be made in relation to the case following the correspondence with the Prime Minister's office. It is also likely that, because of the number of prominent people who were interested in the progress of the Hindujas' naturalisation, further representations would have been made to Home Office Ministers and the Nationality Department. These would have all needed to be responded to. If the case was afforded priority and dealt with expeditiously then the number of such representations would have been reduced. I am therefore satisfied that there were sufficient reasons to justify this case being afforded some priority, as in the case of Mr G P Hinduja.

5.6. During the course of May 1990 routine checks were made of the police and the Security Service. Later in 1990 checks were also made with the Foreign and Commonwealth Office because of some of the details of the case which had come to light. In November 1990 the Nationality Directorate wrote to Mr S P Hinduja requesting consent to contact the Tax Office. This was a standard procedure in respect of self-employed applicants.

5.7. On 25 March 1991 Mr Doug McQueen put forward a submission to Mr Peter Lloyd MP, then Immigration Minister, recommending that both Mr S P and Mr G P Hinduja's applications be refused. (This is covered more fully in Chapter 4, paragraph 4.3 above). This submission was seen by Mr Lloyd and the Home Secretary (Mr Baker) who both agreed with the recommendation. An official in the Nationality Department wrote to Mr S P Hinduja on 18 April 1991 informing him that his application had been refused. This letter only mentioned Mr S P Hinduja's excess absences and made no mention of any doubts about Mr Hinduja meeting the "good character" requirement. (See Chapter 4, paragraph 4.3.)

5.8. Having considered Mr S P Hinduja's first application and having studied the casework papers, I am satisfied that the case was dealt with properly and in accordance with the nationality rules.

The period between Mr S P Hinduja's two applications

5.9. Following the refusal of Mr S P Hinduja's first application for citizenship, a number of Members of Parliament and other prominent people made representations in support of, and enquiries about, Mr G P and Mr S P Hinduja's eligibility for naturalisation. This correspondence is discussed in Chapter 4, paragraph 4.4.

Mr S P Hinduja's second application

5.10. Apart from Mr Vaz's letter of 24 February 1997 to Mr Walmsley, which asked what progress had been made in relation to any applications by both G P and S P Hinduja (see Chapter 4, paragraph 4.5), there appear to have been no further representations or enquiries made in connection with Mr S P Hinduja's eligibility for naturalisation until the contact made between Mr Mandelson, or his private office, and Mr O'Brien, or his office.

The involvement of Mr Peter Mandelson

5.11. The truth about what happened in June or July 1998 and the extent to which Mr Mandelson became personally involved in a query which his private office in the Cabinet Office made to Mr O'Brien or his office has inspired much speculation in the media since Mr Mandelson's resignation as Secretary of State for Northern Ireland on 24 January 2001.

5.12. Although it is with the events of June or July 1998 with which my Review is principally concerned, the terms of reference do require me to review the full circumstances surrounding approaches to the Home Office in connection with the possibility of an application for naturalisation by Mr S P Hinduja in 1998.

5.13. As any contacts between Mr Mandelson and Mr O'Brien, or their offices, form an important part of this element of my terms of reference, I have decided to report my findings in some detail. As mentioned in the Introduction, paragraph 1.6, I have also reviewed the papers and interviewed people who were concerned with this issue in December 2000 and January 2001. This covered the period from 18 December 2000, when Mr Norman Baker MP's Parliamentary Question was being discussed, to 24 January 2001, when Mr Mandelson resigned.

5.14. I have done this not simply out of curiosity. It soon became clear to me that there were discrepancies between the various accounts of what happened in the summer of 1998 and that, in order to attempt to clear-up these uncertainties, it would be necessary for me to review the exchanges which took place in December 2000 and January 2001 between Ministers and the officials in the private offices concerned and in No. 10.

5.15. Because of the events which led to the resignation of Mr Mandelson, much attention has been focussed on the issue of whether a personal telephone conversation took place between Mr Mandelson and Mr O'Brien in June or July 1998. In view of this, I have decided that I must deal with this issue in some detail, although I have concluded that, in itself, the issue is relatively insignificant. Although, even now, I have not been able to establish the exact course of events or even to reach a conclusion with certainty, I have questioned the participants' recollections extensively.

The events of June/July 1998

5.16. When I interviewed Mr O'Brien, he told me that he was certain that he had had a personal telephone conversation with Mr Mandelson about a naturalisation matter concerning Mr S P Hinduja at the end of June or beginning of July 1998. When I interviewed Mr Mandelson, he too said firmly that he did not remember the call and disputed, given the contact between the private offices which had taken place, whether it was reasonable to conclude that an additional personal telephone conversation occurred. I deal with Mr Mandelson's observations in more depth in paragraphs 5.40 to 5.45.

5.17. Apart from his certainty about the call having taken place, Mr O'Brien's other recollections about what happened in June or July 1998 are unclear. This is not surprising, given the time which had elapsed.

5.18. Mr O'Brien told me that he could not recall the exact date of the telephone conversation with Mr Mandelson. He said that his assistant private secretary in 1998, Mr Matthew Laxton, had sent an e-mail about Mr S P Hinduja's interest in naturalisation to Mr Walmsley on 2 July 1998 (the role played by this e-mail is touched on throughout this Chapter). This e-mail had clearly been written as a result of some form of contact from Mr Mandelson or his office, Mr O'Brien suggested, something which has not been disputed by anyone to whom I have spoken, although Mr O'Brien could not recall precisely whether the call had taken place on 2 July itself or shortly before that. The e-mail itself, which is attached at Annex I, does not mention who had raised the issue, when it was raised or how it was raised. This is important to bear in mind because of its significance for later events.

16

5.19. I have been unable to determine with any degree of accuracy the date on which the contacts between Mr Mandelson's and Mr O'Brien's offices took place. As I set out below, none of the private office staff who worked in the relevant private offices in the Cabinet Office and Home Office in 1998 have a clear recollection of the date, although it seems clear to me that, if it took place, it must have been on or before 2 July. This is because, although it is accepted that Mr Laxton's e-mail of 2 July is not, as such, a record of the conversation, if it took place, the e-mail was, clearly, the result of some form of contact between Mr O'Brien and/or his office and Mr Mandelson and/or his office. Mr Mandelson told me that in a five-way "conference call between him, Mr O'Brien, Alastair Campbell and two others on Monday 22 January 2001, Mr O'Brien had said that he recalled that the telephone call with Mr Mandelson had taken place on 28 June 1998, meaning that Mr Laxton's e-mail of 2 July was sent on the Thursday of that same week. Mr O'Brien does not recall saying this (and Mr Campbell corroborates this recollection). I have been unable to verify this comment, but it seems unlikely that it could have taken place on 28 June, because that date fell on a Sunday.

5.20. Mr O'Brien's recollection was that the telephone call with Mr Mandelson lasted about two minutes. Mr O'Brien thought that the conversation began with some brief sociable comment. He then thought Mr Mandelson had said that he had been sitting near an Asian businessman, Mr S P Hinduja, at a recent dinner. Mr O'Brien recalls that Mr Mandelson had said, during the conversation, that Mr O'Brien might recognise the name Hinduja. He did not, although what had recently confirmed in his mind that he had actually spoken to Mr Mandelson was that, during the conversation, and whilst taking notes on a "post it" note, he had spelt Mr Hinduja's name incorrectly. This was something, Mr O'Brien said, which was corrected when he spoke to Mr Laxton, although Mr Laxton does not recall either the "post-it" note or the misspelling of Mr Hinduja's name. Mr O'Brien was not able to tell me with any certainty what subsequently happened to this "post it" note, although Mr O'Brien recalled that it already had writing on it and was, at the time, attached to an unrelated file.

5.21. Mr O'Brien said that Mr Hinduja had told Mr Mandelson that he had heard that the rules or policy for granting naturalisation had changed recently. As described in Chapter 3, paragraph 3.5, around the time of the alleged telephone call, the Government were looking to develop a more positive approach to citizenship. This was set out in chapter 10 of the July 1998 White Paper "Fairer, Faster and Firmer", although there had been no change of rules at the time the alleged telephone call is believed to have taken place or, indeed, since. The Hindujas may have heard about this or they may have become aware of a change of administrative policy in April 1998 which gave greater discretion to officials dealing with naturalisation cases when they examined the passports for date stamps. This followed the removal of embarkation controls and some immigration lawyers had been aware of this.

5.22. Mr O'Brien told me that Mr Mandelson had explained that Mr Hinduja was a prominent man in the Asian business community who had already applied for citizenship and been refused. Mr Mandelson had told Mr O'Brien that

Mr Hinduja would not want to make a further application if there was little chance of success. Mr Hinduja had also been aware that, previously, there had been an issue about the number of days the businessman had spent in the UK, although he did not have the precise details. It appears that these details were later provided to Mr O'Brien's office.

5.23. Mr O'Brien was clear that Mr Mandelson had not made any representations on behalf of Mr S P Hinduja but had tried to establish the Government's policy in this area so that he could relay the details back to Mr S P Hinduja. Mr Mandelson had specifically said that he was not asking Mr O'Brien to grant naturalisation in this case. Mr O'Brien categorically denied that Mr Mandelson had put any pressure on him.

5.24. Mr O'Brien said that Mr Mandelson had initiated the contact but he did not know, when he spoke personally to Mr Mandelson, whether his office had returned a call to Mr Mandelson or Mr Mandelson had telephoned his private secretary and the call was then put through. Mr O'Brien did, though, remember saying to his private office at one point that, if Mr Mandelson telephoned, to put him through.

5.25. Mr O'Brien did not know which of his private secretaries had put the call through to him, or whether a member of his private office was monitoring the call. He also did not know if a note had been made of the conversation by any private secretary.

5.26. Mr O'Brien was not sure what the sequence of telephone calls had been. The most likely scenario, he thought, was that Mr Laxton had spoken to Mr Mandelson, then he, Mr O'Brien, had spoken to Mr Mandelson. Finally, Mr Laxton would have had a conversation with Mr Mandelson's private secretary. Although his memory was unclear about the exact sequence of calls, Mr O'Brien was clear that the conversation with Mr Mandelson had taken place. When I interviewed him a second time, Mr O'Brien told me that he had arrived in the office and remembered somebody telling him that Mr Laxton had spoken to Peter Mandelson. Mr Laxton was not in the office at this point. Mr O'Brien believes that he told his office that, if Mr Mandelson called again, he could be put through to Mr O'Brien.

5.27. Although Mr O'Brien had known Mr Mandelson for some time, and had spoken to him occasionally in the Division Lobby, he did not often get telephone calls from him. This was one of the reasons why he remembered the call. He speculated that Mr Mandelson, because of his higher political profile at that time, would have made a considerable number of calls during the day and might not have recalled this one.

5.28. I spoke to a number of those who worked in Mr O'Brien's private office in 1998. None of them had a clear recollection of how the contact between Mr Mandelson and/or his office and Mr O'Brien and/or his office actually took place.

5.29. Mr O'Brien's private secretary, Mr Jon Payne, told me that he could not remember having made any calls to, or having received any calls from, Mr Mandelson or his private office. Mr Payne did tell me that, shortly after an enquiry had been received from Mr Mandelson or his office, Mr O'Brien had called Mr Payne into his office. Mr O'Brien had explained that he had received an enquiry from Mr Mandelson about Mr S P Hinduja. Mr Payne could not recall how the enquiry had been received or whether Mr O'Brien had said that he had spoken personally to Mr Mandelson but he does remember having the impression, at that time, that the contact had been by way of a personal telephone conversation with Mr Mandelson. Mr Payne said that Mr O'Brien had asked him to deal with Mr Mandelson's enquiry sensitively and to ensure that he gave an accurate answer promptly.

5.30. Mr Laxton, the author of the e-mail of 2 July 1998, remembered that Mr Mandelson's office had telephoned Mr O'Brien's office in 1998. Mr Laxton spoke to a female member of Mr Mandelson's office (Ms Emma Scott has said that this was her) who had told him that Mr Mandelson would like to speak to him. Ms Scott did not recall that she had put Mr Mandelson through to Mr Laxton. She only recalled having two conversations herself with Mr O'Brien's office. The first of these had been generated by Mr Mandelson's office.

5.31. Ms Scott told me that Mr Mandelson had asked her to speak to Mr O'Brien's office around this time in 1998. The reason for making contact was in connection with a query about the naturalisation rules and whether one of the Hinduja brothers was likely to be successful if he re-applied because of the number of days spent out of the country. Ms Scott recalled that she had got an answer back from Mr O'Brien's office. She thought that Mr O'Brien's office had telephoned her back and, so, thought that, in total, two telephone calls had been made. Ms Scott could not remember the name of the person she had spoken to. She remembered that it was a man and thought that she probably spoke to the same person on both occasions.

5.32. Returning to Mr Laxton's account, he told me that, when Mr Mandelson was put through, he had asked Mr Laxton about one of the Hindujas whose previous application for naturalisation had been rejected because of absences from the country. Mr Mandelson wanted to know if there was any point in Mr Hinduja applying again for naturalisation because he had still spent a lot of time out of the country. Mr Mandelson had then said, Mr Laxton told me, that if Mr Hinduja did not have a chance of naturalisation then he would not apply, as it would be embarrassing to be rejected again. Mr Laxton said that, after this initial discussion with Mr Mandelson, Mr Mandelson's office had then provided further details of the number of days Mr Hinduja had spent out of the country.

5.33. Mr Laxton told me that he had informed Mr O'Brien that the telephone conversation with Mr Mandelson had taken place, although he could not recall exactly how he had done this—whether it was by way of a note or a conversation with Mr O'Brien.

5.34. Mr Laxton told me that he did not know if Mr Mandelson had spoken directly to Mr O'Brien on this issue. He did not deny that Mr O'Brien may have mentioned a telephone conversation with Mr Mandelson, but could not remember this.

5.35. The suggestion that Mr Laxton had spoken directly to Mr Mandelson was corroborated by Mr David Barnes, another assistant private secretary in Mr O'Brien's office. Mr Barnes said that he sat next to Mr Laxton in the private office around the time in question and remembered Mr Laxton saying, when he had finished a telephone conversation, something along the lines of "I've just spoken to Peter Mandelson".

5.36. I also spoke to Mrs Lynsey Curtis, Mr O'Brien's then diary secretary and Miss Bryony Morris, an assistant private secretary. Both confirmed that they had no recollection of any telephone call between Mr Mandelson and Mr O'Brien in June or July 1998.

5.37. The recollections of Mr Mandelson's private office at the Cabinet Office in 1998 are also inconclusive. I have already set out the role played by Ms Scott, who recalls one or two conversations with a male private secretary in Mr O'Brien's office, who I have concluded was Mr Laxton. She recalls no personal contact between the two Ministers.

5.38. Ms Maria Daniels, Mr Mandelson's diary secretary, was responsible for monitoring his outgoing telephone calls. Her records, which are only available until 26 June 1998, before, I suspect, the call might have taken place, do not include one to Mr O'Brien. Ms Daniels has no recollection of Mr Mandelson requesting such a call during the period which followed. Mr Rupert Huxter, Mr Mandelson's departing principal private secretary, could recall the question of the telephone contacts being raised but not how they had been handled. He thought Ms Scott's account of what had happened, as she had put it to him, entirely plausible: that Mr Mandelson had mentioned to the private office that he had had a telephone conversation with Mr Hinduja, during which the query about naturalisation had been raised; and that Mr Huxter had then discussed with Ms Scott how to take the matter up with the Home Office in a way which made clear that Mr Mandelson was not making representations. He did not recall any direct contact between the two Ministers.

5.39. Similarly, Mr Mark Langdale, who was replacing Mr Huxter around this time and may have been in the private office during the time in question, had no recollection of any direct contact between the Ministers or their offices on this issue.

5.40. This leaves me with Mr Mandelson's recollections of any contact there may have been with Mr O'Brien or his office about Mr Hinduja's naturalisation. Mr Mandelson told me that he did not remember how the issue had been raised with him by either Mr S P or Mr G P Hinduja. He did not remember any correspondence on this subject at that time and said that he thought that the issue might have been raised informally at a meeting he had had with the Hindujas about some other matters. Equally, they might have telephoned him.

5.41. As I have set out in Chapter 8 below, Mr Mandelson categorically denies that there was ever any link made by the Hindujas between the funding of the Millennium Dome and the question of the naturalisation of either, or both, of the brothers. According to Mr Mandelson, one or both of the Hindujas had asked about a relaxation of Government policy in relation to citizenship and whether it would have any bearing on Mr S P Hinduja's wish to become a citizen of the United Kingdom. Mr Mandelson had told the Hindujas that he did not know the answer to this query but would find out. At this time. Mr Mandelson said, he was not aware of any previous applications by the Hindujas.

5.42.   Mr Mandelson said that his recollection was that, having received the query from the Hindujas, he had asked his private office to find out what the Home Office's response might be. He said that he remembered that Ms Scott had got the requisite information from Mr O'Brien's office but did not recall a personal telephone conversation with Mr O'Brien. Mr Mandelson said that none of the members of his private office recalled a personal telephone call between the two Ministers, which he thought corroborated his account. Mr Mandelson said that it would have been unusual for him to make official calls such as these (i.e. those which were about Government policy or business, and were not personal or political) unless they were facilitated by his private office. He also told me that he did not have a Ministerial telephone directory in his office, so would not have known how to contact Mr O'Brien or his office direct. This is not conclusive as it is possible that Mr Mandelson could have used the No. 10 Downing Street switchboard which would have connected him to Mr O'Brien's office. However, if this had happened, it might have triggered a recollection in the minds of the private secretaries in Mr O'Brien's office, who would have to have spoken to the switchboard operator, as well as Mr Mandelson. They have no such recollection. Mr Mandelson did not discount the fact that he might have mentioned Mr Hinduja to Mr O'Brien in the Division Lobby at the House of Commons. He did not know when such a discussion might have taken place, but it would certainly not have been a substantive one. Mr Mandelson thought that he would have either primed Mr O'Brien to ask his office to expect a call from his, Mr Mandelson's office, about the case, or thanked him for his office's help after the contact in June or July 1998 had taken place. Mr O'Brien did not rule this out. He could not recall such a discussion but thought, that if one had taken place, it would have been after the telephone call and not before it, because he was certain that the discussion on the telephone was the first time the issue was raised personally with him.

5.43.   Mr Mandelson and his representatives thought that there were some inconsistencies in the accounts of those working in the Home Office in 1998 which cast doubt on whether he had had a personal telephone conversation with Mr O'Brien.

—   Mr Mandelson thought it inconceivable that he would have referred to Mr Hinduja as "an Asian businessman whom I sat next to at dinner" in any telephone call in 1998. His association with the Hinduja brothers had been public for some time and was well-known. He said that he would have referred to Mr Hinduja by name in any telephone call;

— Mr Mandelson highlighted the fact that there appeared to be no written record of any conversation between the two Ministers. He also thought it inconceivable that a private secretary would not have listened in to the telephone call given the importance which Mr O'Brien and his office seemed to attach to a personal approach from Mr Mandelson. Mr Mandelson suggested that it was not possible for him to telephone Mr O'Brien direct, without going through the private office and, so, thought it unlikely that a private secretary would not have remembered such a call, and inconceivable that they had not listened in.

— Mr Laxton had said that he did not recall the "post-it" note on which Mr O'Brien had recorded brief details of the call or the suggestion that Mr O'Brien had not spelt Mr Hinduja's name correctly.

— There was also nothing in Mr Laxton's e-mail of 2 July 1998 to suggest that the call had taken place. The e-mail did not refer to any personal contact between the two Ministers and Mr Mandelson did not have to have spoken to Mr O'Brien for Mr Laxton to have got the information he needed to send his e-mail.

— Finally, Mr Mandelson said that he did not understand why he would have needed to speak personally to Mr O'Brien about Mr S P Hinduja's naturalisation, something which Mr Mandelson had regarded to be inconsequential, if he had already got the information he required from Mr O'Brien's private office. There was no reason to think that he would have got any more information out of a personal conversation with Mr O'Brien than he, or his private office, had obtained from Mr O'Brien's private secretary.

5.44. Given Mr Laxton's clear recollection that he had spoken to Mr Mandelson personally, and the corroboration provided by Mr Barnes, I asked Mr Mandelson for his views on whether it was possible that he had spoken directly to Mr Laxton.

5.45. Mr Mandelson told me that this was conceivable, although he could not be sure that such a conversation had taken place. Mr Mandelson said that it was sometimes his practice, if he was in his private office, to take the telephone receiver from a private secretary in order to explain the details of an issue direct with an official who would have the information he required. Mr Mandelson thought that he recalled Mr Laxton's name, which suggested that it was possible that a conversation with Mr Laxton had taken place, although Mr Mandelson could not actually remember it. Ms Scott did not remember Mr Mandelson taking the telephone receiver away from her in this manner. She did not rule it out but did not think that it was his usual practice to speak to an official in another Department in this way.

The events of 2000-2001

5.46. Having reviewed peoples' recollections and the scant documentation which related to the events of June and July 1998, I decided to establish whether the events of the period from 18 December 2000 to 24 January 2001 threw any additional light on what had happened two and a half years before.

5.47. The alleged telephone call between Mr O'Brien and Mr Mandelson resurfaced in 2000-2001 as the result of a written Parliamentary Question (PQ) by Mr Norman Baker MP which was due for answer on 18 December 2000. The PQ had asked the Secretary of State for the Home Department:

> "what representations he has received on the applications by G P Hindiya (sic) and S P Hindiya (sic) for British citizenship from (a) the Right Honourable member for Hartlepool and (b) the Honourable member for Leicester East.".

5.48. The first draft reply which was put forward by Mr Andrew Walmsley did not include Mr Mandelson's name because it was clear to Mr Walmsley that any contact which Mr Mandelson had had with Mr O'Brien or his office had not been representations. Mr Mandelson's interest in the case of Mr S P Hinduja had though been included in the background note. Mr Walmsley's draft reply read:

> "I presume the Hon Member is referring to the applications for naturalisation made by Mr G P Hinduja and Mr S P Hinduja.
>
> No representations have been received concerning the application from either the Right honourable Member for Hartlepool or the honourable Member for Leicester East although the latter did make a telephone enquiry of an official of the Immigration and Nationality Directorate regarding the progress on Mr S P Hinduja's application."

5.49. In respect of Mr Mandelson's involvement, the background note said:

> "There have been no direct representations concerning these applications from the Rt Hon Member for Hartlepool (Mr Mandelson). I understand that Mr Mandelson did speak to Mr O'Brien in 1998 about the general circumstances surrounding the refusal of Mr S P Hinduja's application . . . I do not consider the enquiry to be representations on the application.".

A copy of the full background note is at Annex J.

5.50. I asked Mr Walmsley why he had assumed that there had been personal contact between Mr O'Brien and Mr Mandelson in 1998. Mr Walmsley told me that he had first heard about Mr Mandelson's interest in the naturalisation of Mr S P Hinduja in a telephone call from Mr Payne. He said that Mr Payne had told him that Mr O'Brien had had a telephone call from Mr Mandelson or his office. Mr Walmsley could not remember whether Mr Payne had said that the call had been from Mr Mandelson or from Mr Mandelson's office.

5.51. When Mrs Barbara Roche MP, the Minister answering the question, referred the answer and the background note to Mr O'Brien on about 18 December, he immediately told his assistant private secretary, Mr Varun Uberoi, that he recalled a telephone conversation with Mr Mandelson on this matter in 1998. In the next couple of days, Mr O'Brien said that he had had separate conversations with both Mrs Roche and Mr Straw in which, he said, he was definite in recalling the Ministerial telephone conversation with Mr Mandelson and that there was nothing improper in the content of the conversation. The outcome is contained in Mr O'Brien's note of 20 December 2000 to Mrs Roche (Annex K). This set out:

> "Peter Mandelson requested information on how an application might be viewed under the Home Office policy of encouraging citizenship, but as far as I recall, did not make representations asking that the application be granted.".

There also appears to have been some discussion between the three Home Office private offices about whether to refer to prominent politicians from other parties who had made representations on behalf of the Hindujas. The Home Secretary, Mr Straw, resolved the debate by accepting official advice that other people should not be included because their names were not in the public domain. At that point the second paragraph of the draft answer had read:

> "Two Members made enquiries about the cases. The Honourable Member for Leicester East about when a decision could be expected in the cases, and the Rt Honourable Member for Hartlepool about how an application might be viewed given the Government's wider policy of encouraging citizenship from long-standing residents who fulfilled the criteria.".

5.52. Mr Straw told me that the Parliamentary Question folder arrived with his office before Christmas 2000. Ms Jane Fowler, his assistant private secretary, thought that she had shown Mr Straw the answer on 20 December 2000.

5.53. After discussing the answer with Mrs Roche and Mr O'Brien a form of words was agreed upon. Mr Straw said that he asked for the answer to be faxed over to Mr Vaz's and Mr Mandelson's private offices, which was his normal practice when other Ministers were mentioned in a draft reply. It appears that this was done on 20 December 2000. Mr Straw had told his office to tell Mr Vaz's and Mr Mandelson's that if either of them wanted to discuss this issue with him, then he would be available in the Lobby that evening.

5.54. On 21 December, Ms Fowler said, she received a manuscript note which the Home Secretary had written which said that Mr Keith Vaz had told him that prominent Conservatives had also made representations about the naturalisation of the Hinduja brothers. Ms Fowler said that the Home Secretary then sought advice from Home Office lawyers on whether or not he could name the other people who had made representations, in addition to Mr Vaz or Mr Mandelson. The initial answer to this was provided by Mr Alan Underwood in his submission of 8 January. Further advice followed in Mr Underwood's submission of 23 January (Annex L). This provided a

> "strong health warning on the disclosure of names listed in my earlier note as having an interest in the naturalisation applications of S P and G P Hinduja . . . The names must be in the public domain; otherwise we need their consent.".

This advice was relevant to the answering of a second PQ from John Cryer MP:

> "To ask the Secretary of State for the Home Department what representations he has received from the Right Honourable Member for Bexleyheath and Sidcup and Dame Angela Rumbold concerning the naturalisation applications of S P and G P Hinduja.".

Clearing the PQ with the Northern Ireland Office

5.55. Ms Fowler faxed the answer to the Northern Ireland Office private office on 20 December 2000. This is corroborated by Mr Mandelson's private secretary, Ms Sarah Todd, who said that she had received a telephone call from the Home Secretary's office and Ms Fowler had faxed the draft answer to the Northern Ireland Office. Ms Todd said that she may have had some contact with the Home Secretary's office a couple of days earlier. She recalled that, in December, there had been a rush to get the Question answered before the House of Commons rose on 21 December.

5.56. She said that she had put the answer into Mr Mandelson, because she thought that it needed to be cleared by him personally. In response, he had asked her why it was necessary to answer the question "in this way." Mr Mandelson said that he had not made representations. He did not consider that any involvement he had had in matters relating to Mr S P Hinduja's naturalisation constituted representations.

5.57. She had then spoken to the Home Secretary's office to pass on Mr Mandelson's comments. The urgency had now been taken out of the situation because a holding reply had been given. Ms Todd said that she told Mr Mandelson this and he had asked her, on a copy of the original draft answer (Annex M):

> "Sarah find out what/how/when I raised this with Jack. I can't remember.".

5.58 Mr Mandelson told me that this comment suggested that he had thought that he had raised the matter with the Home Secretary rather than Mr O'Brien. If he had recalled a conversation with Mr O'Brien at that point, he said, then he would have asked his private office to find out about that rather than any conversation or contact with Mr Straw. Mr Mandelson told me that, at that point, he would have dealt with the draft reply in December 2000 without devoting too much attention to it, but thought his response indicated that he had wanted to find out what the facts were before he had agreed to the answer being tabled as it had been drafted.

Into 2001

5.59. After Christmas 2000, Ms Todd spoke to Ms Fowler, again, on or around 10 January 2001. Ms Todd wanted to provide Mr Mandelson with an answer to his question about how he had raised this matter with the Home Office. Ms Fowler had said that the PQ was "live" again and suggested that Ms Todd should speak to Mr O'Brien's office because they would know about any queries Mr Mandelson might have raised with their Minister in connection with Mr S P Hinduja. Ms Todd spoke to Mr Uberoi. Mr Uberoi told me that this took place on 8 January. As a result of these calls Ms Todd wrote Mr Mandelson a note on 11 January which she put in to Mr Mandelson. The note (Annex N) said:

> "I'm told that you (Mr Mandelson) raised the issue with Mike O'Brien either in a telephone call or a personal note. Mike O'Brien does not remember how precisely you raised it but he does remember you asked how an application for citizenship by the Hinduja brothers might be viewed given the positive contribution their work makes to the country. As your exchange with Mike O'Brien was during the time you were Minister Without Portfolio, the only record that exists is the attached copy of an e-mail from Matthew Laxton (Mike O'Brien's Private Secretary) to an official in the Home Office. The e-mail was in response to your query and it makes no reference to you by name." .

5.60. In his evidence to this Review, Mr Mandelson has highlighted that Ms Todd's note of 11 January 2001 seemed to cast doubt on whether Mr O'Brien could recall the nature of the contact with Mr Mandelson or his office in 1998, although by 22 January when the five-way conference call took place, Mr O'Brien's recollection that there had been personal telephone contact was clear.

5.61. I spoke to Mr Uberoi about this. He did not know why Ms Todd had used the words she had in her note of 11 January. Although he did not recall the telephone conversation with Ms Todd very clearly, he was confident that he would not have suggested that Mr O'Brien's communication with Mr Mandelson had taken the form of a "personal note." Mr O'Brien had, probably, on 18 or 19 December 2000, told Mr Uberoi, face-to-face, that he had had a telephone conversation with Mr Mandelson in 1998. Mr Uberoi told me that his discussion with Mr O'Brien took place between 18-20 December 2000. Mr Uberoi was therefore clear in his own mind that the contact had been by way of a telephone call. Ms Todd told me that she had taken care to note what Mr Uberoi had said, given that her purpose in making the call was to try to establish how Mr Mandelson had raised the matter. She was absolutely clear that reference had been made to a telephone call or a personal note. Mr Uberoi told me that he did not discuss this issue with Mr O'Brien on 11 January.

5.62. Ms Todd told me that, as Mr Mandelson was in London on 11 January, she faxed her note of that date to Ms Kirsten McFarlane in the private office in London. Ms McFarlane put Ms Todd's note of 11 January into Mr Mandelson and asked if he was

"content with the attached draft answer?"

His response, which came out of his Ministerial Box on 12 January, was a manuscript "no".

5.63. Mr Mandelson believed that any contact he may have had with Mr O'Brien had not constituted representations. Ms McFarlane had told Ms Todd that Mr Mandelson had said that he might have spoken to Mr O'Brien, in passing, in the Lobby, but he, Mr Mandelson, did not believe that this constituted making representations. Ms Todd told me that Mr Mandelson had maintained from the outset that he had not made representations. She said that Mr Mandelson's immediate reaction to the idea of any contact with the Home Office was that he had thought that he had raised the matter with Mr Straw rather than Mr O'Brien and had also thought that any conversations had taken place in the House of Commons rather than over the telephone. Ms Todd also said that Mr Mandelson had not said, in December 2000 or January 2001, that any contact with the Home Office about Mr S P Hinduja and naturalisation had been only at private secretary level.

5.64. Ms Todd then conveyed Mr Mandelson's views to Ms Fowler. They agreed that, as they were unable to resolve the matter themselves, they would arrange a conversation between Mr Straw and Mr Mandelson.

5.65. Mr Straw recalled that Ms Fowler had told him that she thought he should speak to Mr Mandelson direct about the PQ as the private offices had been unable to resolve the matter. He had agreed to do so. Mr Straw did not have an opportunity to speak to Mr Mandelson over that weekend (13/14 January 2001). On Tuesday 16 January Ms Fowler brought the PQ file into Mr Straw's office and lined up a telephone call with Mr Mandelson. The revised answer had already been faxed to Mr Vaz's and Mr Mandelson's private offices.

5.66. Mr Straw said that he opened the conversation with Mr Mandelson with a discussion about Northern Ireland. Mr Mandelson did not remember that this was how the call had started although he thought that this was quite conceivable. They had then moved on to discuss the Parliamentary Question. Mr Straw had said that the Question had to be answered. A lot of time had elapsed since the Question had been tabled and Mr Straw thought that the matter was quite straightforward. Mr Mandelson told me that he agreed with this account.

5.67. Mr Mandelson had told Mr Straw that he had not made representations on this case, but had made enquiries. According to Mr Straw's account, (I deal with Mr Mandelson's in paragraph 5.71 below), Mr Mandelson had asked why it was necessary to mention him at all in the answer. Mr Straw said he was surprised by this as he thought that Mr Mandelson had to be mentioned in the answer. Mr Straw said that he had told Mr Mandelson that he thought that the answer to the PQ needed to be as accurate and complete as possible.

Mr Straw said that it was his policy to answer Parliamentary Questions in a way which were as complete as possible. Mr Straw told me that he did not understand why Mr Mandelson was so concerned about being included in the answer.

5.68. Mr Mandelson told me that, on 16 January, he had been keen to deal with the PQ and get it answered as soon as possible. The reason why Mr Mandelson had queried why it was necessary to mention him at all in the answer was first, because the Norman Baker PQ had asked about representations and Mr Mandelson had not made any representations. He had not expressed support or endorsement. Second, at this stage of his limited involvement in this matter, no application had been made by Mr S P Hinduja. Mr Mandelson said that he knew Mr Straw had wanted to be as forthcoming and open as possible so Mr Mandelson said that he had agreed to Mr Straw's suggestion that Mr Mandelson be mentioned in the answer to the PQ without further demur.

5.69. Mr Straw had agreed that Mr Mandelson had not made representations about the merits of the application and was happy to revise the answer to reflect this.

5.70. Mr Straw told me that, during this telephone conversation on 16 January, Mr Mandelson had said that he had no recollection of the conversation with Mr O'Brien, but did not deny that it had taken place. Mr Straw had told Mr Mandelson that he, Mr Straw, had spoken to Mr O'Brien about this, he thought, in December 2000. Mr O'Brien confirmed that a telephone call had taken place. Mr Straw said that Mr Mandelson did not make an issue of this and did not regard his failure to recall the telephone call as proof that the call had not taken place.

5.71. Mr Mandelson thought that Mr Straw's account had given me the impression that the telephone conversation which took place on 16 January 2001 was much longer than it actually was. Mr Mandelson said that the conversation had been brief and there had been no substantive discussion of the alleged 1998 telephone call with Mr O'Brien. Mr Mandelson thought that Mr Straw may have made a very short assertion that there had been a telephone conversation between him, Mr Mandelson, and Mr O'Brien in 1998 which he, Mr Mandelson, said he could not remember. Mr Mandelson was prepared to accept that the contact with Mr O'Brien had been mentioned during the course of this telephone call although he now recalled that, during the course of the conversation on 16 January, Mr Straw may not have mentioned that it had been a telephone conversation; he may just have referred to a general contact with Mr O'Brien.

5.72. Mr Straw also thought that Mr Mandelson's office had been told about the Home Office's belief that there had been a telephone call between Mr Mandelson and Mr O'Brien by Ms Fowler before Christmas 2000. This was certainly her recollection. Mr Mandelson denied this and, indeed, Mr Mandelson's belief on 21/22 December 2000 that he had raised this matter with Mr Straw, rather than Mr O'Brien, seemed to suggest that, even if his office had been told about the telephone call in December 2000, he had not been.

5.73. Mr Straw said that, during the conversation with Mr Mandelson on 16 January, there had been some discussion about other MPs making representations on behalf of Mr S P Hinduja. By that time another PQ had been tabled by John Cryer MP, asking about the involvement of other MPs. Mr Mandelson had suggested that the PQs from Mr John Cryer MP and Mr Norman Baker MP should be answered together, but Mr Straw was clear that Mr Baker's PQ needed to be answered quickly and he could not justify holding off any longer. He was concerned that the Norman Baker PQ had gone unanswered for some time. Ms Fowler, who listened in to the call, confirmed that the PQ from Mr Cryer was discussed. Mr Mandelson denies that he was aware of Mr Cryer's PQ at that point and told me that he did not refer to it in the telephone conversation with Mr Straw.

5.74. Mr Straw and Ms Fowler confirmed that Ms Fowler had listened in to the telephone conversation between Mr Straw and Mr Mandelson on 16 January. She did not take a note of the discussion, but had noted the changes which had to be made to the PQ. After the telephone conversation, Ms Fowler had then typed up the answer and sent it over to Mr Mandelson's and Mr Vaz's private offices. The Question was answered on 18 January 2001.

5.75. In the course of this Review I have also discovered that Mr Straw recalls a second conversation with Mr Mandelson in which the contact with Mr O'Brien in 1998 was mentioned. Mr Straw was not able to say when exactly the conversation took place. He has looked at his diary for the period in question, and concluded that the conversation must have happened after Christmas 2000. Mr Straw's recollection is that he spoke to Mr Mandelson in the Lobby— although he thought it was also possible that it might have happened at No. 10, in the margins of a meeting.

5.76. Mr Straw's recollection is that Mr Mandelson approached him in the Lobby and initiated a conversation about the Norman Baker PQ. Mr Straw explained that he remembered this discussion because Mr Mandelson had said, more than once, that he did not see why he should be mentioned in the PQ answer. Mr Straw told Mr Mandelson that Mr O'Brien had a clear recollection of having had a conversation with Mr Mandelson about Mr S P Hinduja in 1998. Mr Straw recalled that Mr Mandelson's reaction was along the lines of "Did I?". Mr Mandelson told me that he could not recall a second conversation and thought that he would have remembered it had it taken place. Also, he was in Belfast or France during much of that week and was unlikely to have voted in the House of Commons.

The "private" comment

5.77. The only other issue relating to the Norman Baker PQ which needs to be set out in this Report is a difference of view between the Home Office and Northern Ireland Office about whether, in December 2000 or January 2001, Mr Mandelson had acknowledged a telephone call with Mr O'Brien and told his private office that this had been "private." If such a claim were true, it would, of course, seriously undermine Mr Mandelson's contention that his dealings with Mr O'Brien's office were done entirely through his private office, even if he accepts that he might have spoken to Mr Laxton during a contact which had been initiated by his private office.

5.78. The suggestion that Mr Mandelson had used the word "private" in connection with any contact with Mr O'Brien was put forward by Ms Fowler who, Mr Straw acknowledged, had passed the information on to him. This allegation was then passed on to Mr Powell and then the Prime Minister by Mr Straw on 24 January 2001, the day Mr Mandelson resigned from the Government. The significance, or otherwise, of this is touched on in paragraph 5.129.

5.79. Ms Fowler told me that during the course of one of her discussions with Ms Todd, Ms Todd had said that she had spoken to Mr Mandelson and he had acknowledged that his conversation with Mr O'Brien had been "private" and so he did not want this conversation mentioned in the reply to the Parliamentary Question.

5.80. I put this suggestion to Ms Todd. She told me that she did not remember herself, or Ms McFarlane, using the words private or confidential in connection with any contact Mr Mandelson had had with Mr O'Brien. This is corroborated by Ms McFarlane. Ms Todd said that she could see how Ms Fowler might have reached the conclusion that any conversations were private, as she, Ms Todd, would have passed on Mr Mandelson's view that any contact with Mr O'Brien may have been a discussion in the Lobby, but Ms Todd could not remember using the word private.

5.81. Ms Todd said that Mr Mandelson had not told her that he wanted any contact with Mr O'Brien kept confidential. This view was corroborated by Ms McFarlane. Mr Mandelson told me that as, at that point, he had not acknowledged that a telephone conversation with Mr O'Brien had actually taken place, he was not likely to suggest that such a call would have been private.

5.82. When I put this issue to Ms Fowler again, she said that she was adamant that the word had been used although she could not recall whether this had been before or after Christmas 2000.

5.83. I am unable to come to a clear view as to whether the words "private or confidential" were ever used in this context. It is significant that Mr Mandelson categorically denies that he ever used either of these words. I return to this issue in paragraph 5.209.

From The Observer to the resignation

5.84. Initially, I was reluctant to review the events which immediately preceded Mr Mandelson's resignation from the Government. Although they had generated considerable media comment, it seemed to me that they fell outside my terms of reference. My scrutiny of the earlier events in December 2000 and

January 2001 suggested, however, that the events of the week beginning 22 January 2001 could have an important bearing on whether I would be able to decide whether Mr Mandelson had personally intervened in June or July 1998.

5.85. The PQ from Norman Baker was answered on Thursday 18 January 2001. The following Sunday, The Observer carried a story with the headline (Annex O):

> "Mandelson helped Dome backer's passport bid.".

The story linked Mr Mandelson's interest in Mr S P Hinduja's naturalisation application with the brothers' donation to the Faith or Spirit Zone in the Millennium Dome. Mr Mandelson told me that, on Saturday 20 January, the day before the article was published, his Special Adviser in the Northern Ireland Office, Mr Patrick Diamond, had telephoned Mr Mandelson. Mr Diamond had said that The Observer were asking Mr Mandelson to clarify what his involvement had been in relation to Mr S P Hinduja's naturalisation application following the answer to the Norman Baker PQ. It was clear that The Observer were trying to link the naturalisation application and the donation of money for the Dome. Mr Mandelson told me that he did not want to appear evasive and so told Mr Diamond to give The Observer some background information which would help to set out what Mr Mandelson saw as his very limited involvement in Mr Hinduja's interest in naturalisation. Mr Mandelson had particularly wanted to get across to The Observer that the enquiries about naturalisation had been handled in the normal way on the official network and that he had not supported an application or made any representations.

5.86. The Observer reported Mr Mandelson's statement:

> "To the limited extent I was involved in this matter I was always sensitive to the proprieties. The matter was dealt with by my private secretary. At no time did I support or endorse this application for citizenship.".

This statement was to go on to play a significant part in the rest of that week's events, particularly when, later in the week when Mr Mandelson thought that there was some documentary evidence to support the existence of the telephone call, he had acquiesced in the view that a call had taken place.

5.87. Mr Campbell told me that he had first seen the story in The Observer on the Saturday night (20 January 2001). He had telephoned his office to see if there had been much interest in the story from the media, which there had not. During the course of Sunday 21 January when media enquiries came in, Mr Campbell said that he wanted to check the facts of the story.

5.88. Mr Campbell said that he put a telephone call through to Mr Mandelson on the afternoon of Sunday 21 January. Mr Campbell said that it was clear that Mr Mandelson was heavily involved in matters in Northern Ireland and was also exercised by a story running in that day's Sunday Times with the headline:

> "Mandelson caught in fresh feud with Brown over election planning.".

When asked how he should respond to any press queries about The Observer article, Mr Mandelson told Mr Campbell to refer to the statement given to The Observer. (This is consistent with Mr Mandelson's account.) After the telephone call Mr Campbell spoke to the Downing Street Duty Press Officer to ensure that this line was deployed.

5.89. In his comments to me, Mr Mandelson maintained that his account to The Observer was not misleading. When the statement was given to The Observer, Mr Mandelson had had one or two conversations with Mr Straw the previous week when the 1998 telephone call was mentioned by Mr Straw. However, as suggested in paragraph 5.208, Mr Mandelson maintained that these references were fleeting and, at that time, he had his mind very much on the important and fast-moving events in Northern Ireland and did not attach the significance to the references to the 1998 call which they attracted the following week. At the time he spoke to The Observer, I do not believe that Mr Mandelson was aware of the possibility that he had spoken to Mr Laxton. I understand that he was only reminded that this may have happened when he saw an account of Mr Laxton's interview with me in connection with my Review.

5.90. In relation to his statement to The Observer, Mr Mandelson told me that The Observer had wanted to know about any links between sponsorship of the Dome and naturalisation applications by the Hindujas. The newspaper did not seek details of any telephone calls which may have taken place between the Home Office and the Cabinet Office in 1998. This account is confirmed by Mr Diamond.

5.91. Mr Mandelson said that his firm recollection was that he had tasked his private office with the query from Mr Hinduja and they undertook to find out the information required. Mr Mandelson accepted that he may have spoken to Mr Laxton, although he was now sure that he did not speak to Mr O'Brien. The reason why the statement to The Observer was worded in the way it was, Mr Mandelson told me, was in order to emphasise that the prime mover behind any discussions with the Home Office in relation to Mr Hinduja's naturalisation application was Mr Mandelson's private office of the time. Mr Mandelson had wanted to make it clear that any query was dealt with officially, using Civil Servants, and not through political channels. Mr Mandelson said that he was also trying to give The Observer a crisp comment so that they would be more likely to print it in full, rather than edit it.

5.92. Mr Mandelson concluded that The Observer statement was not only consistent with his version of events but also those of Mr O'Brien and Mr Straw, both of whom maintained that at all times contacts between the Home Office and Cabinet Office in 1998 had been made through official channels. To say that the matter was handled by private secretaries was therefore consistent with all three accounts of the events even if Mr Mandelson had made a personal intervention at some point and had spoken to Mr Laxton. This explanation is important in view of the significance that The Observer article had for later events.

5.93. On Monday 22 January, in Mr Campbell's view, the story did not really take off. It had not been included in television broadcasts although some of the newspapers included articles on it.

5.94. During the Lobby briefing at 11 am on 22 January, Mr Campbell said that he repeated the line he had agreed with Mr Mandelson, that all dealings with Mr O'Brien's office were done through Mr Mandelson's private office. Mr Mandelson pointed out to me that Mr Campbell's line had changed because he used the words

> "Mr Mandelson had not got involved in the matter beyond being asked to be involved—which he had refused to do. Instead, he had asked his Private Secretary to refer the issue to the Home Office.";

which had not been the words Mr Mandelson had given to The Observer.

5.95. During the afternoon of 22 January, Mr Smith gave his answer to the House of Commons. Mr Mandelson told me that at lunchtime that day Mr Smith had been looking for a line to take at oral questions that afternoon. Mr Mandelson had suggested that he should emphasise that the application had been dealt with in the usual way. In the event, Mr Smith told the House of Commons:

> "I understand that Mr Hinduja's passport application was dealt with in the normal way, by the normal people, under the normal terms. My Rt Hon Friend's (Mr Mandelson's) then Parliamentary Private Secretary told Mr Hinduja that that would be the case. That was my Rt Hon Friend's sole involvement. He had no involvement in endorsing or supporting the applicant at any stage.".

5.96. Subsequently, this answer was believed to be misleading as it referred to Mr Mandelson's sole involvement being through his "Parliamentary Private Secretary". (The reference to the Parliamentary private secretary was in fact incorrect as Mr Smith had referred to Mr Mandelson's private secretary and this was misreported in Hansard. I understand that the bound version of the Official Report will correct this. Mr Mandelson had maintained that the matter had been dealt with by his civil service private secretaries.) Mr Mandelson told me that the words "sole involvement" had, in fact, been added to that day's line to take by No. 10 rather than by him.

5.97. At the 4 pm Lobby briefing on 22 January, conducted by his deputy, Mr Campbell said, the story was not even raised.

5.98. The reason why the story was resuscitated, was because later on that day (22 January), Mr Campbell told me, some lines to take were sent over from the Home Office which, Mr Campbell thought, had reported:

> "Mr Mandelson made verbal enquiries to the Minister".

It would have appeared that this was the line to take which would be deployed by the Home Office Press Office and which might already be in the public domain. In response to reading this suggestion that Mr Mandelson had spoken to Mr O'Brien personally Mr Campbell telephoned Mr Mandelson. He said that he had a problem in that a new line to take from the Home Office was suggesting that Mr Mandelson had made verbal representations. Mr Campbell told me that Mr Mandelson did not know what that was referring to. He did not recall it.

The Conference Call—22 January 2001

5.99. Mr Campbell had then spoken to Mr O'Brien and subsequently set up a conference call involving himself, Mr Mandelson, Mr O'Brien, Mr Godric Smith—Mr Campbell's deputy—and the Northern Ireland Office Director of Information, Mr Tom Kelly. I have heard accounts of this call from the three main protagonists.

5.100. Mr Campbell told me that, during the conference call, Mr O'Brien had been emphatically clear that there had been a conversation and that nothing improper had happened. At that point, Mr Campbell thought that Mr Mandelson had immediately seen the presentational difficulties of the contradiction with the version of events in the public domain. Mr Campbell said that Mr O'Brien was clear about what had happened. The general view of the participants in the conference call was that the matter now needed to be sorted out and a correct version of events put out.

5.101. The conference call had been arranged for early to mid-evening and, Mr Campbell said, Mr Mandelson had had to leave it early because he was at a dinner with the Chief Constable of the Royal Ulster Constabulary and thought that he had kept him waiting long enough. Mr Kelly remained on the line. By then, Mr Campbell said, Mr Mandelson had agreed that there was a need to correct the record in the morning. Mr Campbell told me that, during the conference call, Mr Mandelson's basic position had been that if Mr O'Brien recalled it so clearly then he had to assume that it had happened.

5.102. Mr O'Brien confirmed that Mr Mandelson had been in the middle of a dinner with the Chief Constable of the Royal Ulster Constabulary and had said that he had not recalled the conversation with him, Mr O'Brien, in 1998. Mr O'Brien told me that Mr Mandelson had said that as he, Mr O'Brien, was confident that the conversation had taken place then he was happy to accept that, but he still did not recollect it. Mr O'Brien told me that the conference call on 22 January had taken place before he, Mr O'Brien, had been made aware that Mr Straw had also spoken to Mr Mandelson the week before and mentioned the alleged 1998 telephone call. Mr O'Brien said that he did not think that Mr Mandelson was being deceitful but that his contention that he could not recollect the call was genuine.

5.103. Mr Mandelson's recollection is that, during the course of the conference call, Mr O'Brien had said that the telephone call he remembered having with Mr Mandelson had taken place on 28 June 1998. Mr Mandelson said that he had challenged Mr O'Brien about his memory of the telephone call in 1998. Mr O'Brien's recollection of the discussion had been clear, Mr Mandelson said, but, during the conference call he had developed the impression that Mr O'Brien's memory was supported by a record of the conversation.

Mr Mandelson said that Mr Campbell had also, later, given the impression that such documentation existed and said that he had had it read out to him. Mr Mandelson said that Mr Campbell had suggested that the existence of some record of the telephone conversation would cause Mr Mandelson problems. Both Mr O'Brien and Mr Campbell deny that they had said that there was a record of the telephone conversation.

5.104. Mr Campbell told me that he would not have been aware of any record of the telephone call at that point on the Monday evening. At that stage, all Mr Campbell was aware of, he told me, was the line to take which had come from the Home Office, which had referred to verbal enquiries and Mr O'Brien's clear recollection. Mr O'Brien pointed out to me that Mr Mandelson should have already known that no documentary proof existed, other than Mr Laxton's e-mail, because this had been explained to him in Ms Todd's note of 11 January 2001 (Annex N).

5.105. Mr Mandelson said that he recalled being told on 22 January that documentary proof of the call existed and his belief that there was documentary proof was why he had conceded that the call, which he still maintained he did not recall, had taken place. It was also why, during his briefing of the media on 23 January 2001, he had taken this line and why he had agreed to Mr Campbell correcting the Lobby the next day.

5.106. After the conference call, Mr Campbell said that he had passed on to the Prime Minister what he thought was the correct version of events. Mr Campbell said that, in his view, the contents of the conference call had established that a call had taken place in 1998. He did not look for a record to corroborate it because he had no reason to disbelieve Mr O'Brien and Mr Mandelson had said that he had to assume that the call had taken place. This was a key point in the confusion which was building up. An important part of the explanation of the reason why he, Mr Mandelson, conceded that a call had taken place in 1998 was because he thought that there was documentary proof that it had happened, which there was not. Equally, he suggested that Mr Campbell and his colleagues had not looked to verify whether any record existed because Mr Mandelson had confirmed that the telephone call must have taken place.

5.107. Also on the evening of 22 January, Mr Jonathan Powell, the Prime Minister's Chief of Staff, had asked the Secretary of the Cabinet, Sir Richard Wilson, for advice on what line the Prime Minister should take at Prime Minister's Questions on Wednesday 24 January about Mr Mandelson's actions in relation to the citizenship applications by the Hindujas. Sir Richard told me that although Mr Powell wanted Sir Richard to find out what he could about the facts, he expressly asked him not to undertake any kind of investigation. Mr Powell asked for the advice by the following evening. Sir Richard told me that he had telephoned Mr Joe Pilling, Permanent Secretary at the Northern Ireland Office, and asked him to speak to Mr Mandelson to establish Mr Mandelson's version of events. Mr Pilling had done this. I understand from

Mr Mandelson that although he spoke to Mr Pilling he does not recall being consulted on the drafting of the account which was given to Sir Richard Wilson. Sir Richard also spoke to Mr John Warne, Acting Permanent Secretary at the Home Office, to ask for that department's version of events. Shortly afterwards, Mr Richard Abel, Sir Richard's principal private secretary, spoke to the Department of Culture, Media and Sport for the same purpose.

Tuesday 23 January

5.108. Mr Campbell told me that he had spoken to Mr Straw before briefing the Lobby again on Tuesday 23 January. At that Lobby briefing Mr Campbell had said that Mr Mandelson's office had had a chance to look at the facts on their offices' first working day after the weekend during which a telephone call had come to light. Mr Mandelson says that he had agreed that the Lobby should be re-briefed but had not cleared the exact words which Mr Campbell intended to use. The Lobby briefing, which had been agreed with Mr O'Brien and Mr Straw said that:

> "Mr Mandelson's office had been able to look at the records in full . . . (they) had discovered that he had had a very brief telephone conversation in June 1998 with Mike O'Brien which had been set up by their two Private Offices. Although Mr Mandelson had no recollection of the call, clearly it had taken place and he had therefore asked him (the PMOS) to make that clarification here and now. However, it did not change the material fact that he had done nothing improper.".

5.109. The story now began to take off again and, according to Mr Mandelson's account, on the advice of the No. 10 Press Office, he agreed to do a number of media interviews. Mr Campbell, however, told me that his recollection was that the No. 10 Press Office had not advised Mr Mandelson, but had "agreed" with this course of action. Mr Mandelson told me that, after the Lobby briefing on 23 January, he could pursue no other course of action but to support Mr Campbell's revised account. During his briefing of the media on 23 January, and in particular in an interview with Channel 4 News, he had insisted that he had not forgotten anything. He did this because he wanted to demonstrate that he had not forgotten what he did not know to be the truth in the first place. Mr Mandelson told me that even at that stage he was as certain as he could be that the conversation with Mr O'Brien had not taken place. Despite the stimulus of the events of that time, he still could not recall the telephone conversation.

5.110. In parallel, on Tuesday 23 January, Sir Richard Wilson began to sketch out his minute to the Prime Minister. He gave the first draft, including the principles which should apply in cases such as this, to his office when he arrived at work. In the course of that day, Sir Richard told me, his private office spoke to various Government Departments to discuss the draft minute in order to flesh it out. The draft had been cleared for factual accuracy with the Departments concerned, including the Northern Ireland Office. Sir Richard had completed the minute and sent it forward to No. 10 that evening.

5.111. As this document shows (see Annex P), Sir Richard had concluded on the basis of the material he had seen that the Prime Minister could reasonably argue in public that no one had produced any evidence that Mr Mandelson had done anything improper in connection with the naturalisation applications. He suggested that a Minister making an enquiry of another Minister in the way which was alleged would have been acting properly provided of course that there was no suggestion of it being done in return for a favour, either to the Government or to the Minister in a private capacity. In the more slippery area where a Minister was dealing separately with the individual concerned, care would be needed to avoid misinterpretation. But even forwarding an application for naturalisation, which had not happened in this case, might have been appropriate.

5.112. As long as the Home Office acted properly in processing an application for naturalisation, in accordance with the criteria, anyone, including a Minister, could make what comments they judged suitable, provided that they were disinterested. If the application had been handled differently by the Home Office because of the interest of a Government Minister, then, Sir Richard thought, that would have been a matter of concern. In this case, it needed to be established that there was no link between the naturalisation query and any other matters, such as the funding of the Dome.

5.113. Sir Richard told me that on the evening of 23 January he had had no indication from the material he had received from the Home Office, DCMS and the NIO that there had been any such link, and this was recorded in his minute to the Prime Minister. It had been understood at that point, he said, that he had not carried out an investigation.

5.114. In terms of the alleged telephone call between Mr O'Brien and Mr Mandelson, Sir Richard said that, on 23 January, no-one involved seemed to be in doubt that a telephone call had taken place. At that point Mr Mandelson seemed to have acknowledged that he had made a call and was understood to have agreed that the matter should be clarified in the press. Mr O'Brien was clear that the call had taken place.

5.115. Sir Richard had concluded that the Prime Minister could argue publicly that no-one had produced any evidence that Mr Mandelson had done anything improper. This was his view when it was suggested late in the evening of 23 January that there should be an Inquiry. He agreed, however, to be ready with proposals for an Inquiry the following morning if that was what was decided.

5.116. On the evening of 23 January 2001, after Sir Richard's minute had been sent to the Prime Minister, Mr Mark Langdale, previously one of Mr Mandelson's private secretaries in the Cabinet Office, sent a minute to Mr Richard Abel. The minute said that Mr Langdale had spoken to Ms Scott, the assistant private secretary in Mr Mandelson's private office who had dealt with the enquiry about Mr S P Hinduja, and that she believed that Mr Mandelson and Mr O'Brien had spoken personally over the telephone in 1998.

5.117. Mr Langdale told me that he spoke to Ms Scott again on 25 January and that it became apparent during the course of that discussion that there had previously been a misunderstanding. Ms Scott had not meant to give the impression that Mr O'Brien and Mr Mandelson had spoken to each other personally as that was not her recollection. Mr Langdale corrected the record in a further note to Mr Abel on 26 January. Ms Scott told me that she had not spoken to Mr Mandelson between her initial conversation with Mr Langdale and Friday 26 January and had, therefore, not spoken to him before her second conversation with Mr Langdale on 25 January.

5.118. In terms of the significance of Mr Langdale's minute, I have established that it was only seen by Sir Richard Wilson and Mr Abel. It served only to confirm in Sir Richard's mind the perception, which had already been created, that the telephone call had taken place in 1998. It was not in the dossier of papers which, I understand, the Prime Minister had in front of him the next day

The evening of 23 January 2001

5.119. The Tuesday evening seems to have been a time of some activity when the Prime Minister appears to have made a number of telephone calls to Mr Mandelson and Mr Straw.

5.120. As well as speaking to Mr Campbell and the main protagonists about the events of 22, 23 and 24 January, I also spoke to Mr Jonathan Powell and Ms Clare Sumner, a private secretary to the Prime Minister. As a result of these discussions I have drawn together the following chronology of the events of the Tuesday evening.

5.121. At 8.05 on the Tuesday evening, the Prime Minister telephoned Mr Straw. The Prime Minister had wanted to know if Mr S P Hinduja's citizenship application had been dealt with correctly, and generally wanted to establish the facts. Mr Straw said that he had not seen any of the official papers and submissions relating to Mr S P Hinduja at that time and had not therefore influenced the process of Mr Hinduja being granted naturalisation. Mr Straw had said that the process had been dealt with by Mr O'Brien and officials.

5.122. During this telephone call it seems that Mr Straw had told the Prime Minister that he had spoken to Mr Mandelson on two occasions and had reminded Mr Mandelson that he had spoken personally to Mr O'Brien in 1998. This may have been the first time the Prime Minister had heard this. Mr Campbell could not recall whether or not he had previously mentioned conversations which had taken place between Mr Straw and Mr Mandelson on this issue. Mr Straw also suggested to the Prime Minister that it was possible that Mr S P Hinduja's case had been prioritised because of the queries from Mr O'Brien.

5.123. The next call between the Prime Minister and Mr Straw was later on that evening. By this time, the Prime Minister had also seen Mr Walmsley's submissions of 14 August 1998 (on Mr S P Hinduja), 3 July 1997 (on Mr G P Hinduja) and 12 October 2000 (on all three brothers). The Prime Minister was concerned with how the Home Office had responded to Mr O'Brien's approval of the 14 August 1998 submission and how Mr S P Hinduja's solicitors had been told that Mr Hinduja should apply for naturalisation.

5.124. During this second call with Mr Straw, the Prime Minister asked Mr Straw if the official dealing with the case of S P Hinduja (Mr Walmsley) had known about Mr Mandelson's involvement. Mr Straw had assumed that he had.

5.125. I was told by Ms Sumner that the Prime Minister had three telephone conversations with Mr Mandelson that evening. During one of them, the Prime Minister had said that a key question was the apparent conflict between what Mr Mandelson had said to The Observer on Saturday 20 January and his conversation with Mr Straw the previous week when Mr Straw had made it clear that Mr O'Brien had a recollection of a telephone call between himself and Mr Mandelson in 1998.

The day of Mr Mandelson's resignation: Wednesday 24 January 2001

5.126. On the following morning, I understand that Mr Straw told the Prime Minister that his private office had also spoken to the Northern Ireland Office private office at some point and had said that Mr O'Brien recalled speaking to Mr Mandelson in 1998.

5.127. Sir Richard Wilson had been called to see the Prime Minister in his flat shortly after 9am on the Wednesday morning. There were five people already there as well as the Prime Minister, and Lord Irvine arrived shortly afterwards.

5.128. The Prime Minister told Sir Richard that he had spoken to Mr Straw, the previous evening, who had told him about the telephone calls he, Mr Straw, had had with Mr Mandelson the previous week. The meeting was told that it now appeared that despite being reminded by Mr Straw about the telephone call with Mr O'Brien, Mr Mandelson had let No.10 and Mr Chris Smith believe that he had had no personal contact with Mr O'Brien, and that as a result Mr Smith had unintentionally misled Parliament.

5.129. Ms Sumner and Mr Powell told me that Mr Powell had been telephoned by Mr Straw that morning when Mr Straw had mentioned that his private office had been told by a private secretary in the Northern Ireland Office that Mr Mandelson had said that his conversation with Mike O'Brien in 1998 was "private". Mr Powell said that he relayed this information to the Prime Minister but by that time the meeting had moved on.

5.130. At that meeting on the morning of 24 January, I understand that the Prime Minister had before him a dossier of papers including Sir Richard's minute, the e-mail of 2 July 1998 from Mr Laxton to Mr Walmsley, and Mr Walmsley's three submissions about the Hindujas' naturalisation applications. Sir Richard told me that the Prime Minister did not appear to have any Home Office papers which linked the naturalisation applications with the funding of the Millennium Dome.

5.131. After the Prime Minister had left the discussion to attend another meeting, there followed some discussion about the figures relating to Mr Hinduja's absences from the UK. During the meeting Mr Straw had been asked by telephone about these figures and Mr Straw had asked Mr O'Brien about their origin. Mr O'Brien had apparently said that the figures had been given to his private office by Mr Mandelson's office during one of the telephone calls in 1998. There had been concern that the figures in the e-mail were the same as the figures which were given in a submission to Mr O'Brien in August 1998. People had wondered whether the figures were right and had been independently checked.

5.132. During the discussion, those present had also wanted to establish whether the naturalisation applications of the Hinduja brothers had been treated, by the Home Office, in the same way as comparable cases. It had been thought necessary to find out whether or not the Hindujas' applications had been dealt with any differently because Mr Mandelson had approached Mr O'Brien, or whether their applications had been approved because of their contribution to the Dome.

5.133. What followed that meeting on the morning of 24 January has been very widely reported and commented on. Mr Mandelson met the Prime Minister at No. 10 and tendered his resignation.

Follow up to the Alleged Telephone Call

5.134. This narrative now returns to June or July 1998. Following the discussion with Mr O'Brien about Mr S P Hinduja's interest in naturalisation, Mr Walmsley told me that Mr Payne had telephoned him and explained that there had been some contact with Mr Mandelson, who had wanted to know what Mr S P Hinduja needed to do in order to be successfully granted naturalisation. Mr Walmsley recalled that he told Mr Payne that Mr Hinduja had been refused naturalisation in 1991 because he had not met the unwaivable requirement that he had to be in the United Kingdom on the day which began the five year qualification period. Mr Walmsley thinks that he may have had two telephone conversations with Mr O'Brien's office in connection with this enquiry. I do not think that that is an important detail.

5.135. The next development was Mr Laxton's e-mail (Annex I) to Mr Walmsley of 2 July 1998. The role played by this e-mail in the events of December 2000 and January 2001 has already been covered. Mr Laxton does not recall how much time elapsed between the contact with Mr Mandelson and his office and the sending of the e-mail. Mr O'Brien's view was that it was Mr Laxton's habit to process such work quickly.

5.136. Mr Laxton's e-mail is interesting, because it does not name Mr Mandelson, even though I am satisfied that the e-mail was written following an enquiry from Mr Mandelson or his office. Mr Walmsley confirmed that he was aware of Mr Mandelson's interest in the case, because it had been mentioned to him by Mr Payne during their earlier conversation or conversations. Mr Laxton's explanation for not including Mr Mandelson's name in the e-mail was that enquiries about immigration and nationality issues were usually received in letter form, rather than by way of a telephone call. The MP's name would, of course, be on the letter head and, so, the identity of the MP making the enquiry would be clear when the letter was sent to the Immigration and Nationality Directorate for advice. This had not been the case with Mr Mandelson because the enquiry had not been received in writing. Mr Laxton said that he did not recall Mr O'Brien asking him to keep Mr Mandelson's name out of the e-mail. This is consistent with my understanding that Mr Payne had already told Mr Walmsley about Mr Mandelson's interest. If Mr O'Brien had wanted the contact kept a secret, he would have asked Mr Payne not to reveal Mr Mandelson's identity either. Mr Laxton's e-mail very firmly put the enquiry about Mr S P Hinduja's naturalisation in the context of Mr O'Brien's wish to see a more positive approach to citizenship; something which was set out in Chapter 10 of the White Paper "Fairer, Faster and Firmer" later in July 1998 (see Annex E).

5.137. One point about this e-mail which came to light in the discussions which took place in No. 10 on 24 January 2001, was that the number of days which the e-mail reported that Mr S P Hinduja had spent out of the United Kingdom in the preceding five years was identical to the total number of days contained in Mr Walmsley's submission of 14 August 1998 (see below). The submission was the official response to the 2 July 1998 e-mail—see paragraphs 5.140 to 145 below for consideration of this submission.

5.138. I asked Mr Walmsley whether or not he had checked the figures which were provided by Mr Mandelson's office independently or whether he had taken them on trust. He told me that because of his previous dealings with Richard Hoare, Mr Hinduja's solicitor, he had assumed that the figures were correct. Because Mr Hoare had compiled the list of absences for Mr G P Hinduja's 1997 application for citizenship and they were correct, Mr Walmsley said that he had no reason to believe that the figures for Mr S P Hinduja would be incorrect. Mr Walmsley told me that he had got the figures independently from Mr Hoare as well as from Mr Mandelson's office, via Mr Laxton, and that the figures were the same. He also said that he suspected that the figures given to him by Mr Hoare would have shown higher absences than IND's calculations because the Nationality Department/Directorate tended to count the days on which an applicant was travelling to and from the United Kingdom as days when they were present in the country. Applicants and their legal advisers tended to count arrival and departure days as time spent out of the country. Mr Walmsley also thought that, at that time, it would have been unwise to rely on passports as categorical proof, because it was no longer common practice to have embarkation stamps put in passports. It would have been necessary therefore to corroborate the passports with other evidence in order to confirm absences from the United Kingdom. (This account is consistent with the letter which he had sent about the effects of the change of practice on embarkation controls which I refer to in Chapter 3.)

5.139. Finally, Mr Walmsley said that the number of days Mr S P Hinduja had spent out of the country was not a crucial matter (see paragraph 5.180) and the decision to grant citizenship had not turned on whether Mr S P Hinduja had spent a few more or a few less days out of the country than his solicitor had claimed he had. Other factors, such as the fact that Mr S P Hinduja appeared to have had "thrown in his lot" with the United Kingdom were more important.

The Submission of 14 August 1998

5.140. The next development was Mr Walmsley's submission of 14 August 1998 (Annex Q) which was the official response to the e-mail of 2 July 1998. I understand that Mr O'Brien's office enquired about the whereabouts of this submission earlier in August 1998 because Mr O'Brien was keen to clear any outstanding work before he went on leave later that month.

5.141. Mr Walmsley's submission of 14 August recommended that Mr O'Brien should:

> ". . . indicate to Mr Hinduja that we would be inclined to look favourably on his application, provided he is resident in the UK for tax purposes, and suggest that his solicitor gets in touch with me.".

Strangely, there is no draft letter for Mr O'Brien to send to Mr Mandelson or Mr S P Hinduja or any suggestion as to how he might communicate this news to Mr Hinduja. This might be explained by the fact that the submission was put forward on the day Mr Walmsley went off on leave and may have been prepared in something of a rush (see below).

5.142. The submission explains Mr Hinduja's large number of absences from the UK (819 days) and gives the reasons for the refusal of Mr Hinduja's application in 1991: the days spent out of the country in that five year period; and some doubts about Mr Hinduja's ability to meet a requirement to be of "good character". This latter point is touched on very briefly in the submission. It says:

> "These (the terms of meeting the "good character" requirement) centred on a reported Inland Revenue investigation of their tax affairs and their alleged part in the Bofors scandal in India which concerned excessive commissions paid to the Indian Government of Mr Gandhi by the Swedish firm. These were, however, resolved concerning Mr Gopichand Hinduja's application and there is no reason to believe that Mr Srichand Hinduja would not now meet the requirement.".

Mr Walmsley did not again consult the South Asian Department of the FCO before putting forward his submission of 14 August 1998, despite the fact that it was now some 21 months since he had last consulted them. In view of the importance and sensitivity of the alleged involvement of the Hinduja brothers with the Bofors affair, I think that he should have checked again with the FCO. Had he done so, he might have learned that, in January 1998, in another important well-publicised development in the case in India, the Indian authorities investigating allegations concerning the award of the Bofors contract had sent Letters Rogatory, via the United Kingdom Central Authority in the Home Office, to the Attorney General for Guernsey, for information concerning bank accounts there which they thought might have been used to deposit corrupt payments. It is not clear that any of the accounts which they wished to investigate were accounts held for the benefit of Mr G P and Mr S P Hinduja, but both brothers were mentioned in the Letters Rogatory as being amongst those who were being investigated. Had Mr Walmsley known about this information, he would, presumably, have drawn it to Mr O'Brien's attention in his submission of 14 August 1998. Whether it would have led to a different view being taken about the "good character" requirement must be a matter of speculation, but it would, at least, have been a relevant consideration.

5.143. There is some dispute about when Mr O'Brien saw this submission—either before he went on leave or some time afterwards—but Mr O'Brien is clear that he ticked and initialled the submission and indicated that he was content with the recommendation. I have been unable to track down a copy of the initialled submission or any written response from Mr O'Brien's office which indicates that the Minister was content, but this seems consistent with the general lack of record keeping which has been a feature of this Review.

5.144. One curious feature about the submission was that, unlike the submissions of 3 July 1997 and 22 June 2000 on Mr G P and Mr Prakash Hinduja respectively, the submission of 14 August 1998 did not contain a copy list. The copy of the submission which is on the file seems to suggest that a copy only went to Mr O'Brien. This is an unusual practice for the Civil Service, where submissions on sensitive issues, such as this, tend to be copied to a wide range of colleagues, including, sometimes, the relevant Secretary of State and Permanent Secretary, as well as other members of the Department, the Special Advisers and the Press Office. The fact that this submission was not copied at least to some others in the Home Office was considered unusual by all the people I asked. I mentioned this point to Mr Walmsley, because I needed to satisfy myself that the lack of a copy list, when combined with the fact that Mr Laxton's e-mail did not mention Mr Mandelson and the later inconclusive suggestion from Ms Fowler that Mr Mandelson wanted his contact with Mr O'Brien kept private, did not suggest that Mr Mandelson and Mr O'Brien were trying to be secretive about their contact in relation to Mr S P Hinduja.

5.145. Mr Walmsley told me that as 14 August 1998 was his last day before going on leave, he may have omitted a copy list inadvertently, in his rush to clear all outstanding work. When I showed him a copy of the submission, Mr Walmsley seemed genuinely surprised at the lack of a copy list. He also suggested that he may have e-mailed copies of the submission to other people, but not highlighted this on the submission itself. I have been unable to confirm this, but have no reason to disbelieve Mr Mandelson's or Mr O'Brien's statements that they had not asked for the contact in 1998 to be kept a secret. I do not think that there is anything sinister about what happened.

Mr O'Brien's Letter of 5 October 1998

5.146. On 5 October 1998, Mr O'Brien wrote to Mr Mandelson (Annex R). This letter has taken on a certain significance during the course of this Review, not least because there appeared to be no record of it in the Home Office—in Mr O'Brien's office or the Nationality Directorate. A copy finally came to light because, in 1998, Mr Mandelson had sent a copy to Mr S P Hinduja who had sent it to Mr Vaz's constituency office, who had then forwarded it to No. 10, following the events of January 2001.

5.147. Mr Jonathan Caplan QC, on behalf of Mr Mandelson, suggested to me that the letter's opening sentence contained extraordinary wording if there had been personal contact between Mr O'Brien and Mr Mandelson in 1998. The letter began:

> "You may recall that you were in contact with my office last month concerning Mr S P Hinduja who is considering submitting an application to naturalise as a British Citizen.".

Mr Caplan's contention was that the letter would have referred to the personal contact, rather than contact with Mr O'Brien's office, if personal contact had taken place. The reference to "last month" is also odd, as the contact with Mr O'Brien or his office, took place, as far as I have been able to establish, in June or July, rather than September 1998. I comment later on this point.

5.148. I had originally thought that a draft of this letter may have been attached to Mr Walmsley's submission of 14 August 1998 and become detached. This was not the case. The draft letter was not referred to in Mr Walmsley's submission and Mr Walmsley told me that he did not draft the letter, although clearly it is an official draft rather than one written by Mr O'Brien personally. Although I have been unable to corroborate this, my suspicion is that the draft letter was written by someone in Mr O'Brien's office in August 1998 as the reference to "last month" was not changed when it was given to Mr O'Brien for signature. I have been unable to confirm this though and Mr O'Brien has no recollection of the letter.

How Mr S P Hinduja's Application Was Processed

5.149. Following Mr O'Brien's letter of 5 October 1998 to Mr Mandelson, Mr S P Hinduja reapplied for naturalisation on 21 October 1998, on a copy of his original application form. The original application form was faxed to Mr Hinduja's solicitor by Mr Walmsley on 20 October 1998. The form was then re-signed and re-dated and sent back to the Nationality Directorate the next day.

5.150. I queried whether it was the usual practice to allow an applicant to resubmit a previous, unsuccessful, application form. It would appear that the British Nationality Act 1981 does not require the use of an application form, but a number of the people I spoke to in the Nationality Directorate in Liverpool thought this lawful but unusual, and told me that the usual practice was to require the completion of a fresh application form. I put this point to Mr Walmsley. He assured me that this practice was not unusual and should be seen in the context of the Nationality Directorate wanting to offer applicants a swift and helpful service, saving them the effort of having to fill in a new application form. There were clear pressures to reduce delays when dealing with naturalisation cases and, in order to meet the targets which had been set, Mr Walmsley said that caseworkers had developed a number of shortcuts which allowed them to process cases, still thoroughly, but more quickly. One of these shortcuts was a tendency not to take up references on an applicant mainly because this was of minimal value. Referees tended to make complimentary comments about an applicant. If they were not likely to do this, then they would not usually be chosen as a referee. Given this practice, there seemed little point in requiring Mr S P Hinduja to fill in a second application form, even if his referees had changed. All the other details had remained the same, I was told.

5.151. In resubmitting the form, Mr S P Hinduja also attached his schedule of absences from the United Kingdom over the previous five years. As I have said above, these accorded with the figures given by Mr Mandelson's office to Mr O'Brien's in 1998 and Mr Walmsley checked them independently with Mr Hinduja's solicitor. Although the schedule of absences was submitted, it was not accompanied by passports for the five-year period covering 21 October 1993 to 21 October 1998. This may have been because, in line with Mr Walmsley's comments in paragraph 5.138, he had developed a working relationship with Mr Hinduja's solicitors and so trusted them. Also, he did not consider the exact number of days' absence from the country to be a key issue when it came to taking the decision to grant citizenship.Additionally, the schedule only covered the period up until 6 January 1998 and not up to the date of application. Again, this may not have been so important given Mr Walmsley's view that the other matters relating to the application were in order. It would have been preferable though if the schedule of absences had covered the full five-year period.

What Other Checks Were Made?

5.152. Mr Walmsley then began processing the case. I will come to issues of why Mr Hinduja's case was given priority and why he was granted citizenship despite his absences from the country in paragraphs 5.166 to 5.182. What I deal with in this section is some irregularities in the processing of the case which I have discovered during the course of my Review.

The Unwaivable Requirement

5.153. First, there is the issue of whether or not Mr S P Hinduja met the unwaivable requirement in the British Nationality Act 1981 that an applicant must have been physically present in the United Kingdom at the beginning of the five year qualification period. Mr S P Hinduja's application was signed on 20 October 1998, but was not received by the Nationality Directorate until the next day. This would have meant that Mr S P Hinduja would have needed to be in the United Kingdom on 22 October 1993 to qualify.

5.154. There is a certain lack of clarity about whether Mr S P Hinduja met the unwaivable requirement. The records of the Nationality Directorate suggest that Mr Hinduja was not in the United Kingdom between 15 September 1993 and 26 October 1993. Mr Walmsley assured me though that he was satisfied that Mr S P Hinduja met the unwaivable requirement before he granted naturalisation.

5.155. Although this suggests an irregularity, I do not think that it is a major point. If he had thought it an issue, Mr Walmsley could have told Mr S P Hinduja's solicitors to delay the application until 25 October 1998, so that he met the requirement of being in the United Kingdom on 26 October 1993. This would have made no material difference to the application other than to have delayed it a few days.

Further Checks

5.156. A further issue which I needed to look into was why Mr Walmsley had not made any further checks with the police, the Foreign and Commonwealth Office or the Security Service in 1998.

5.157. A police check was made on Mr S P Hinduja in relation to his application in 1991. In terms of why a further check had not been made in 1997, Mr Walmsley told me that the police were finding it increasingly difficult to process the volume of checks in relation to nationality cases at around this time. As a result, Mr Walmsley said, the Immigration and Nationality Directorate had reduced the number of police enquiries which were made.

5.158. It might also have been the case that, as Mr Walmsley had been in regular contact with Mr S P Hinduja's solicitor and because any major police interest in the Hindujas might have been reported in the newspapers, he, Mr Walmsley, could be fairly confident that there would be no trace on the police records.

5.159. Mr Walmsley told me that he did not go back to the Security Service in 1998 or 1999 because, by the end of 1998, the Security Service were becoming less active in nationality cases and it was decided by Ministers only to check with the Security Service records in the case of applicants of particular national origins. These were not relevant in the case of Mr S P Hinduja.

5.160. My comments on Mr Walmsley's decision not to request any further information from the Foreign and Commonwealth Office are set out in paragraph 5.142.

5.161. A letter from the Inland Revenue was not requested to confirm Mr S P Hinduja's tax details. I asked Mr Walmsley about this. He told me that there was no statutory requirement to ask the Inland Revenue about an applicant's status, but it could be a consideration in determining whether or not an individual met the requirement to be of good character. The Inland Revenue had been consulted in 1991 in relation to Mr G P Hinduja's first application, and this showed that he was not under investigation. Mr Walmsley said that, in 1998, there was no reason to believe that Mr S P Hinduja was trying to evade his tax requirements. His residence in the United Kingdom would not have allowed him to claim that he was not resident in the United Kingdom for tax purposes, and Mr Walmsley told me that, in view of the circumstances and his own experience, there was nothing to be gained from making further enquiries of the Inland Revenue.

5.162. Finally, there is no file copy of a letter which the Nationality Directorate should have sent to Mr S P Hinduja concerning the fee for processing the naturalisation application. This request would normally have been made when requesting documents, during the initial consideration of the case. It is clear though that Mr Hinduja paid the fee, and so I must speculate that the request for the fee was made over the telephone.

The Granting of Naturalisation

5.163. On 17 March 1999, Mr S P Hinduja signed his Oath of Allegiance and, on 23 March 1999, Mr Walmsley signed the print which granted Mr S P Hinduja's naturalisation. It was usual practice for officials to deal with matters such as this. In the normal way, Ministers were not consulted or informed that naturalisation had been granted.

Prioritisation and the Residence Requirement

5.164. There are two particular aspects of the way in which Mr S P Hinduja's application was processed which have attracted considerable comment since the case became highlighted in January 2001. These were:

— why Mr S P Hinduja's case was dealt with so quickly; in particular, whether Mr Hinduja's contribution to the Dome and Mr Mandelson's limited involvement had afforded him any priority; and

— why Mr S P Hinduja was granted naturalisation despite the fact that, according to his own records, he had spent 819 days out of the country. This compared with Mr G P Hinduja's 540 days and the norm in the British Nationality Act 1981 of 450 days.

5.165. I will take these points in turn.

47

Prioritisation

5.166. In Chapter 3 I touch on some of the reasons why priority might be given to an applicant's naturalisation application. In Chapter 4 I have set out the reasons why Mr G P Hinduja's application was given priority. Many of the same reasons are relevant in the case of Mr S P Hinduja.

5.167. At Annex D I attach a copy of the caseworkers' guidelines. These spell out some of the circumstances in which an applicant can be afforded priority. Broadly, these include cases where a mistake in the Nationality Directorate has inconvenienced an applicant; where refusal of priority would create significant additional work for the caseworkers; or when an applicant is deserving of such priority. In this last category are included refugees, the elderly and people unable to make journeys necessary for compassionate or business reasons on existing documents, as well as cases where an applicant wishes to represent the United Kingdom in a sporting event. On the face of it, the case of Mr S P Hinduja does not fit easily into any of these categories although, because of the number of prominent people who, in the past had made representations or enquiries on his behalf, it could be argued that a decision not to grant priority could have resulted in extra work. This would be because any letters of support or enquiries about progress would all need to be answered and Ministers advised accordingly.

5.168. In the light of this, I was interested to tease out the reasons for the decision to grant priority in this case. In my discussions with Mr Walmsley, and also with some of his colleagues, I identified a number of reasons for this decision in addition to the expectation that possible further representations or enquiries might have been received if consideration of the case was delayed.

5.169. First, as was the case with Mr G P Hinduja's second application, Mr Walmsley had much of the necessary information at his disposal and so swift consideration of the case was a distinct possibility. With many applications for naturalisation, I was told, caseworkers often needed to go back to applicants to obtain the rest of the information they needed for their consideration of the case. Clearly, much of this had been compiled for Mr S P Hinduja's initial application in 1991 and so any possible delays here were already overcome.

5.170. Another observation which I heard was that when applicants had hired solicitors to deal with their case, the initial information which was sent to the Nationality Directorate was often much more complete than if an applicant was acting for themselves. This would be because the solicitor would be well-practised in the requirements of the Nationality Directorate and was able to compile, and forward, a full set of papers which might take some time to get from an individual applicant who was unfamiliar with this area of law. I find this explanation plausible.

5.171. A second reason for the case being prioritised was the fact that Mr Walmsley had dealt with the case himself. Most nationality casework was dealt with at a more junior level than Mr Walmsley. This meant that any new cases would automatically be added to the work being processed by that officer unless there were special reasons to expedite the case in line with the caseworkers' guidelines.

5.172. At the time when Mr S P Hinduja's application was processed, Mr Walmsley was the Director of the Nationality Directorate, a Grade 6 Civil Servant. Mr Walmsley told me that because he was very experienced in nationality policy, he tended to deal with high profile cases by himself rather than delegate them to more junior and less-experienced colleagues. This was borne out by the fact that Mr Walmsley had dealt, at around the same time, with other high-profile applications for citizenship which had attracted media attention and which needed to be brought to the attention of Ministers. I suspect that part of the reason for this was because Mr Walmsley did not want to expose what he saw as his more inexperienced colleagues to the pressures of dealing with Ministers and media attention. Again, this seems plausible.

5.173. Clearly the case of Mr S P Hinduja was high profile and had already attracted the attentions of a number of prominent people. Mr Walmsley knew that he would have to expose his analysis to Ministers—as he did—and so decided to process the case himself.

5.174. As a more senior Civil Servant therefore, Mr Walmsley did not have the same volume of casework to deal with and Mr S P Hinduja's application did not need to join the queue of cases waiting to be processed. Mr Walmsley also told me that, around the time when Mr S P Hinduja's application had been received in 1998, the Nationality Directorate was undergoing some reorganisation, as it became part of the wider Integrated Casework Directorate within the Immigration and Nationality Directorate. As part of this reorganisation, Mr Walmsley knew that he was about to move to another area of the Home Office, outside Immigration and Nationality, and took the decision to deal with the case of Mr S P Hinduja himself, whilst he was still able to, rather than pass it on to his successor. It was, Mr Walmsley told me, a purely pragmatic decision. I suspect that, as I touch on in paragraphs 5.189 and 5.190, because Mr Walmsley had not minuted the files as completely as he should have done and had not fully set out the reasons behind his decisions he thought it would be easier to deal with the case quickly rather than explain to his successor what his reasoning had been. Finally, Mr S P Hinduja was a prominent businessman and a quick decision on his naturalisation application would have allowed him to travel in and out of the country more easily in order to carry out his business.

5.175. It is self-evident that Mr S P Hinduja's case was dealt with more swiftly than the 20.1 months average at that time for section 6.1 applications. As has been exposed in media comments on this matter, the application was received in October 1998 and consideration was finalised by the following March. Whilst this was unusual, it was not unique. In reply to a Parliamentary Question asked by Mr David Lidington MP, which was answered on 26 February 2001, in 1998 2.1% (468 cases) of all naturalisation decisions were taken within six months. This had increased by 1999 to 5.1% (1,112 cases). By 2000 5.4% (1,371) cases were decided within that timeframe. Because of technical problems the 2000 figure only relates to the months of January and May to December but, nonetheless, illustrates the point that Mr S P Hinduja was not a case apart.

5.176. A further point is that, as I have mentioned earlier, there was a general drive in the Nationality Directorate, inspired by Ministers and senior managers, to deal with cases more expeditiously. In 1997, as the answer to Mr Lidington's question explains, 75% of cases took at least 18 months to complete. By 1998 this had reduced to 43.4% and in 1999 to 20.1%.

5.177. In line with his general philosophy, Mr Walmsley had wanted to be helpful. As he had the requisite information to hand it was possible for him, as a more senior officer, to take the decision to deal with Mr S P Hinduja's case more swiftly than the norm.

Residence Requirement

5.178. As I set out in Chapter 3, the British Nationality Act 1981 contains an expectation that an applicant for citizenship will have spent a certain amount of time in the United Kingdom over the five year period which precedes their application. The norm, mentioned in the Act, was 450 days. Mr G P Hinduja's 1997 application demonstrated that he had spent 540 days out of the country. By his own reckoning—which, as I mention above, might have been on the high side—Mr S P Hinduja's absences stood at 819 days.

5.179. During comment on this case, the view has been expressed that this level of absences was excessive and that Mr S P Hinduja must have been afforded special treatment in order for his naturalisation application to be granted, particularly as his earlier application had been refused on these grounds. My investigations during this review do not necessarily bear this out, for a number of reasons.

5.180. First, during my discussions with caseworkers in the Nationality Directorate, I was given the impression that the residence requirement, although something which needed to be borne in mind, was not necessarily the key factor when it came to deciding whether or not to grant an applicant naturalisation. I understand that, as long as the other requirements of the 1981 Act are met, the caseworkers tended to work on the assumption that absences up to 900 days might be acceptable. This was particularly so if applicants had a valid reason for such a high level of absences, for example, if they were business people who needed to travel extensively, such as the Hindujas, or merchant seamen, international musicians, etc. Absences of over 900 days would tend to be unusual and would need to be referred to a more senior officer. In this context, therefore, Mr S P Hinduja's absences do not seem to be excessive.

5.181. There are also precedents of people with high absences being granted citizenship. I was given, as examples:

— a merchant seaman with 1,334 days absence over five years granted citizenship in 1989;

— another merchant seaman with 1,179 days absences granted citizenship in 1992;

— an opera singer with 917 days absences granted citizenship in 1992; and

— a businesswoman with 979 days absence granted citizenship in 1997.

5.182. There are other examples. The reason for outlining this is to demonstrate that, whilstMr S P Hinduja's absences were certainly on the high side, they were not unprecedented. Mr S P Hinduja had, in Mr Walmsley's view, thrown in his lot with the United Kingdom. He and his wife lived in this country and his children went to school here. In the light of this, Mr Walmsley took the view that Mr S P Hinduja's absences, which were due to the nature of his work, were acceptable. This analysis was accepted by Mr O'Brien when he approved Mr Walmsley's submission of 14 August 1998.

5.183. It is also necessary to consider what was happening in policy terms at the time when Mr S P Hinduja's application was considered. There was certainly a significant shift, if not a definite policy change, towards a more positive approach to citizenship. It was this understanding that there may have been a change in nationality policy which might, after all, have prompted Mr S P Hinduja's enquiry in the spring or summer of 1998. Although the actual policy had not changed at that stage, it is clear that the mood of the Nationality Directorate was beginning to change.

5.184. When I spoke to Mr O'Brien, he told me that whilst he was Immigration Minister, he had tried to encourage a more positive attitude to citizenship. He had had meetings with officials about this and had worked closely with these officials on drafting Chapter 10 of the July 1998 White Paper "Fairer, Faster and Firmer".

5.185. Chapter 10 of the White Paper (Annex E) is entitled "Encouraging Citizenship" and outlines a number of ways in which the Government intended to encourage and enhance citizenship. The opening section of paragraph 10.1 says:

> "In the UK "citizenship" normally means more than just the nationality of inhabitants. It also encompasses elements in involvement and participation and sharing of rights and responsibilities.".

5.186. It is paragraph 10.7 which is most important in this context. It is entitled "Residence Requirements" and states:

> "Changes in the operation of the immigration control, in particular to encourage greater flexibility in the form and manner in which leave to enter is granted, may require changes in current residence requirements for citizenship under the British Nationality Act 1981. In addition, many of those who at present cannot satisfy the requirements are those who travel abroad on behalf of firms in this country to drum up business, and thereby contribute to the economic well-being of the country and help create jobs. The Government intends to create a more flexible approach to the residence requirements based upon whether an individual was ordinarily resident in the UK and paying his or her taxes here, the overall length of their residence and connections with this country, and the reasons for their absences.".

5.187. Although there had not been an actual change in policy towards citizenship at this time, Mr Walmsley confirmed that the mood of Chapter 10 of the White Paper very much influenced the way in which Mr S P Hinduja's application was regarded.

The Working Practices in the Nationality Directorate

5.188. Finally, I feel that I should comment on the working practices of the Nationality Directorate in 1998-1999. When I scrutinised the case papers on Mr G P and Mr S P Hinduja, which were held by the Nationality Directorate in Liverpool, it became clear that they were not maintained in the way in which they should have been by Mr Walmsley. In particular, there was a paucity of minutes on the file to explain the reasons why decisions to grant both brothers' applications had been taken.

5.189. I think that this is particularly so in the case of Mr S P Hinduja, where there do not seem to be any minutes explaining why Mr Walmsley had decided to grant the case priority or allow the application despite Mr S P Hinduja's absences. The caseworkers and managers who currently work in the Nationality Directorate commented on the lack of minutes and thought that this was contrary to caseworking good practice. However, they explained that Mr Walmsley was an expert on nationality policy and tended to keep a lot of the reasons for his decision making in his head. As such, they suggested, the lack of minuting did not suggest that Mr Walmsley was being evasive or trying to hide the reasons for his decisions. Instead, it was rather an example of less than perfect administration.

5.190. I put this point to Mr Walmsley. He accepted that the minuting of the flies was not as it should have been. He explained that he would often put his reasons in formal notes or submissions. These would be placed on the file rather than the flysheet minuted, as is the usual practice. Mr Walmsley also said that he was involved in a number of high profile cases at this time, as well as being Director of the Nationality Directorate. Because of the volume of his work and his management responsibilities he tended not to minute the files owing to lack of time, although he admitted that he should have done. Notwithstanding these points I should like to comment that, throughout my Review, Mr Walmsley has been consistently honest and frank about the way in which he had dealt with the cases of the Hinduja brothers and I should like to put on record my gratitude for that.

5.191. As a postscript I should add that, from 1998-1999, a number of measures have been put in place to improve the working practices of the Nationality Directorate. Each team of nationality caseworkers has its own senior team leader who maintains quality of decisions and ensures consistency within the team and throughout the nationality group.

Intelligence Material

5.192. I have had full access to any intelligence material which was held which might be relevant to the terms of reference of my review.

5.193. During the period when the naturalisation applications by Mr G P and Mr S P Hinduja were being handled, the Secret Intelligence Service (SIS) had accumulated a certain amount of intelligence about the Hindujas' business activities abroad. It would not be appropriate for me to describe in detail the nature of this material. Suffice it to say that it raised the possibility that they had been involved in a number of dubious practices, in some cases potentially amounting to illegal activities, but that none of the indications of such involvement was conclusive. The material covered, but was not confined to, the Bofors scandal.

5.194. None of the material was seen by the Home Office, nor was the Security Service aware of it at the time when the Home Office made their routine checks in the course of their consideration of the naturalisation applications of Mr G P and Mr S P Hinduja. This was because the material had been gathered by SIS in response to a request in a different context. SIS's collection of the intelligence had been in accordance with its functions under section 1(2) of the Intelligence Services Act 1994.

5.195. Both the Security Service and SIS are required to use the information which they collect only for the statutory purposes for which they are authorised to collect it. In the case of the Security Service, checks requested by the Home Office in respect of naturalisation are undertaken by the Security Service as part of the Security Service's function of safeguarding national security. No issues of national security were relevant to the consideration of these naturalisation applications so that, even if the Security Service had been aware of the information, it would not have been appropriate for it to pass it to the Home Office. The different context in which SIS's intelligence was gathered also explains why it was not shown to the Home Office.

5.196. Nonetheless, the information available in the Secret Intelligence Service was undoubtedly relevant to the issue of whether the test of "being of good character" in Schedule 1 to the British Nationality Act 1981 was satisfied in the case of the applications from the Hinduja brothers. If this information had been available to the Home Office at the relevant time would it have made any difference to the outcome of the applications for naturalisation? This is, of course, a hypothetical question and, in the case of such an important and sensitive issue, the Home Secretary would have had to be consulted. Any conclusion which might be reached now on this issue must necessarily be tentative but, having inspected the intelligence material personally, my own view is that, because of its speculative and inconclusive nature, the conclusion would probably have been that its existence did not of itself justify a refusal to grant naturalisation. In the case of the material about the Bofors scandal, the Home Office did address that issue, as I have already described earlier in my Report.

Conclusions

Contacts Between Mr O'Brien and Mr Mandelson

5.197. In itself the question of whether Mr Mandelson spoke directly to Mr O'Brien in a telephone call is relatively insignificant. All those involved are at one in saying that at no time did he seek to influence the Home Office in favour of Mr S P Hinduja's case or make representations on his behalf. Its only significance lies in its impact on the events which took place in December 2000 and January 2001, which I have described. Despite the paucity of written records, the hazy and inconclusive recollections of many of those involved and the inconsistencies in the various accounts, although I cannot reach a view with any certainty, the best conclusion which I feel able to reach is that it is likely that a personal telephone conversation involving Mr O'Brien and Mr Mandelson took place in June or July 1998. I have also concluded that there were a number of contacts between the then Ministers' private offices and that it is likely that Mr Mandelson spoke personally to Mr Laxton. This is a possibility which Mr Mandelson has not denied, although he does not actually recollect it. I have, however, found it difficult to establish the exact sequence of these calls or, indeed, how many calls took place in total. Depending on whose account one believes, the number of calls could range from one or two to four or five, although I think it unlikely that as many as four or five separate calls would have been necessary to deal with a relatively straightforward enquiry such as this.

5.198. The main reason why I believe that it is likely that Mr O'Brien and Mr Mandelson spoke to each other over the telephone on this issue in June or July 1998, is the consistent recollections of Mr O'Brien. Indeed I have been impressed with Mr O'Brien's firm and unshakeable recollection of the telephone call. I do not regard the possibility of an additional Lobby contact (see paragraph 5.42) as affecting my conclusion, as recollections are so faint and there is no corroboration.

Mr O'Brien's recollections

5.199. I take their accounts in turn. Mr O'Brien has maintained throughout that the telephone call took place. Mr Payne seems to believe that Mr O'Brien told him about the call just after it had taken place, and, when the PQ by Norman Baker MP was tabled in December 1998, Mr O'Brien was at pains to reveal that he had spoken to Mr Mandelson personally, over the telephone, in 1998. Both Mrs Barbara Roche and Mr Jack Straw emphasised this in their evidence to this Review.

5.200.   I am satisfied that Ms Todd's minute of 11 January 2001 to Mr Mandelson, which said that Mr O'Brien "does not remember how precisely you raised it (Mr S P Hinduja's interest in naturalisation)" (paragraph 5.59) did not accurately record any uncertainty by Mr O'Brien. I have established from Mr Uberoi that Mr O'Brien was not consulted on this point on 11 January 2001. I am not therefore persuaded by Mr Mandelson's contention that the note of 11 January, which has already been subject to some debate in the newspapers, casts any doubt on the general reliability of Mr O'Brien's recollection of the events of June or July 1998.

5.201   I also doubt Mr Mandelson's proposition that it is inconceivable that he would have referred to Mr S P Hinduja as an "Asian businessman whom he sat next to at dinner". Mr O'Brien's recollection of this part of the conversation is very clear but, either way, I do not think that it is an important detail and, again, do not consider it to cast doubt on Mr O'Brien's general recollections. I do not, however, think it entirely inconceivable that Mr Mandelson may have used this description as he would not have known, I assume, whether or not Mr O'Brien was familiar with Mr Hinduja's name and may have referred to "an Asian businessman" to give Mr O'Brien some background or context to the rest of the call. The fact that Mr O'Brien told me that Mr Mandelson went on to name Mr Hinduja, satisfies me that Mr Mandelson was not trying in any way to be underhand or secretive during the course of this discussion.

5.202.   I also do not think that the lack of written documents or personal recollections prove that the call did not take place. The period of time which has elapsed since June or July 1998 would make it suspicious should recollections be crystal clear. In terms of Mr O'Brien, I am willing to believe that the call was of such a nature that he would have recalled its existence two and a half years later, although, even in his case, the supporting details are unclear. In terms of documentation, Chapter 9 sets out my observations on the working practices of the private offices at that time. In terms of my conclusions to this Chapter, suffice it to say that I am not entirely surprised that there is such a paucity of documents or other written records to support the existence of the telephone call. There should have been better records of the call, in both private offices, but I am willing to accept that there were not and that those which might have existed have since been destroyed.

5.203.   I do, though, find it strange that no-one in Mr O'Brien's office in 1998 recalls putting Mr Mandelson through to Mr O'Brien, although I am willing to accept Mr Payne's explanation that it was the usual practice to put calls straight through and not to monitor them. Therefore, a call, even from a senior Minister, may not necessarily have been memorable.

5.204.   I am also satisfied that my inability to trace the "post-it note" on which Mr O'Brien recorded the misspelt name when noting the telephone call, and Mr Laxton's recollection that he could not recall the post-it note, do not mean that it did not exist.

5.205. In sum, therefore, I am satisfied that Mr O'Brien's account has, throughout, been consistent and frank. Also I can see no reason why he would have created and consistently stuck to such a recollection if it had been doubtful or untrue, particularly given the disproportionate consequences for Mr Mandelson of Mr O'Brien's determination to stand his ground.

Mr Mandelson's Recollections

5.206. There has been much speculation in the newspapers recently that I would conclude that Mr Mandelson did not deliberately mislead anyone, be they the Prime Minister, Mr Campbell, Mr Straw or Mr Smith, during the events of December 2000 and January 2001. In this regard, at least, these predictions are correct. I have no reason to doubt Mr Mandelson's honesty throughout this period and am happy to accept that he is genuine in his belief that he does not recall the telephone conversation with Mr O'Brien in 1998, which has now hardened into a view that it did not take place. Throughout his evidence to me, Mr Mandelson has also been consistent and frank. He has consistently maintained to me that he believes that no telephone call took place between him and Mr O'Brien. He has also been consistent in accepting that he may have spoken to Mr Laxton. He has stressed that he only acquiesced in the suggestion that there had been a telephone call during the week beginning 22 January because he felt that he had no alternative in the face of the evidence which he thought had been presented. Accordingly, I do not believe that Mr Mandelson has tried to deceive anyone during the course of these events. I believe that he has found himself at the centre of what he himself has described as a "muddle" which gained momentum at a pace which exceeded the importance of the event in dispute—the existence of a telephone call two and a half years ago.

5.207. I also accept Mr Mandelson's account of why he authorised Mr Diamond to give the statement to The Observer which he did. It was made clear to me that the issue of how contact between the two offices was made in 1998 was not an issue at that point. The issue was whether there had been any connection between the Hinduja brothers' donation to the Dome and their wish to be granted naturalisation. I therefore accept Mr Mandelson's explanation that the statement to The Observer was phrased in the way it was because of his wish to stress that any enquiries about Mr S P Hinduja's interest in naturalisation were processed officially, through his private office, rather than through unofficial political channels. I have discovered nothing to contradict this and do not believe that Mr Mandelson was seeking to be evasive. I do think that Mr Mandelson was concerned that his involvement in making enquiries about Mr S P Hinduja's naturalisation might have been misinterpreted by Members of Parliament and the media and that, when the first draft reply to Mr Baker's PQ was put to him, he was keen to be kept out of the answer. Strictly speaking, this was an accurate response because Mr Baker's Parliamentary Question had asked about representations and it has been clear all along, and no-one has contradicted this, that Mr Mandelson made enquiries not representations. However, I accept his explanation that when Mr Straw explained that Mrs Roche needed to be as open as possible about Mr Mandelson's limited involvement, he accepted this without hesitation or demur.

5.208. I accept Mr Mandelson's explanation of why he had not recalled his conversation or conversations with Mr Straw during the week beginning 15 January 2001, when he was asked, the following week, to give an account of his recollections of a telephone call in 1998. Mr Mandelson was involved in a very important stage of the peace talks in Northern Ireland in January 2001 and I can accept that some passing references to his personal contact with Mr O'Brien (Mr Mandelson does not think that it was stressed at that point that this took place over the telephone) could quite easily have been forgotten by him. Although these conversations may have seemed unimportant at the time to Mr Mandelson who had his mind quite reasonably on other matters, it is clear that they were to assume great significance in the following week. It is not difficult to see how The Observer article, combined with Mr Mandelson's omission to mention the conversation(s) with Mr Straw, may have given the impression that he had not given an honest account of his role. I have been unable to come to any conclusion about whether or not there was a second conversation between Mr Straw or Mr Mandelson.

5.209. I have been unable to come to any definite conclusion about the suggestion that Mr Mandelson wanted his contact with Mr O'Brien kept private. Ms Fowler is adamant about her recollection, and I have no reason to doubt the honesty of this, but similarly Ms Todd and Ms McFarlane deny that such a word was used and I, also, see no reason to doubt their honest belief. I do though find it slightly unlikely that Mr Mandelson's consistent belief that he could not recall a telephone conversation with Mr O'Brien would have turned, in December 2000 or January 2001, into a clear recollection of a contact which must be kept private. I suspect that this was a misunderstanding between private offices on what seemed an unimportant issue, which was being processed at what must have been a busy time.

5.210. Finally, I come to why Mr Mandelson seemed to accept the existence of the call during the conference call on 22 January and why he was content for the Lobby to be briefed accordingly the next day. I think that the reason for this was because Mr Mandelson believed that the evidence which supported the existence of the call was stronger than it actually turned out to be. Mr Mandelson seemed to think that Mr O'Brien and Mr Campbell had documentary proof of the call and that they had told him that. There was none. Both Mr O'Brien and Mr Campbell deny that they gave this impression to Mr Mandelson but I have no reason to doubt the impression which Mr Mandelson had developed. At that point on 22 and 23 January, Mr Mandelson found himself in a difficult position. The answer given by Mr Chris Smith to the House of Commons had been changed by someone other than Mr Mandelson to talk about Mr Mandelson's "sole involvement" and Mr Campbell had told the Lobby on Monday 22 January, as he had agreed with Mr Mandelson, that all dealings with Mr O'Brien's office were carried out by Mr Mandelson's private office. Both of these events put Mr Mandelson in a difficult position on the Tuesday and Wednesday of that week. He had agreed to the record being put straight and then had to hold that line, although, it turned out that the evidence supporting the fact that he had intervened in the matter personally, other than Mr O'Brien's firm recollection, was not as strong as he had previously believed. Indeed it turned out that there was no other evidence.

5.211. All this was clearly a muddle. Events moved very quickly and definitive statements about what had happened in 1998 were made on the basis of evidence which turned out to be incomplete. This was entirely understandable in the light of the attention being focussed on this issue and the need for the Government to be seen to be responding quickly and properly. As a result, the events surrounding the alleged call in 1998 began to assume an importance which they did not deserve.

5.212. There are many issues which have been investigated by this Review which have been important. Except for the events of December 2000 and January 2001, which have great significance for the reputation of the two men involved, the issue of whether or not Mr Mandelson and Mr O'Brien spoke personally in 1998 was not one of them. In my view, both Mr Mandelson and Mr O'Brien behaved perfectly properly in the way in which they dealt with and processed Mr S P Hinduja's query about a possible change in the nationality rules.

Processing of the Naturalisation Application

5.213. As I have said, I am satisfied that Mr O'Brien behaved perfectly properly throughout. Once he had received the enquiry from Mr Mandelson—however that was done—he passed the matter on to his private office, who handled the matter in the normal way.

5.214. I do not think that there was anything suspicious about the fact that the Home Office did not have a record of Mr O'Brien's letter of 5 October 1998 to Mr Mandelson. I suspect that the letter was drafted by Mr O'Brien's private office and that any record of it held in the Private Office was destroyed, along with all the other papers from this time. I accept Mr Caplan's point that the letter could have been more happily drafted if it had referred to direct contact with Mr O'Brien, if such contact had taken place. But I do not think that I can conclude that the drafting of this letter proves that there were no such contacts. I think it is equally plausible that the letter was drafted less than precisely and it must be remembered that there is no dispute that there were contacts between the private secretaries.

5.215. I am also satisfied that throughout his very limited involvement in Mr S P Hinduja's interest in naturalisation Mr Mandelson behaved entirely properly. He passed the issue on to the Home Office in the appropriate way and played no further role in the matter, apart from forwarding the letter of 5 October 1998 to Mr S P Hinduja. I am also satisfied that Mr Mandelson did not try to influence Mr O'Brien or his officials at any point and did not make representations on behalf of Mr Hinduja's application.

5.216. In terms of the handling of the application in the Nationality Directorate I have reached the following conclusions.

5.217. As I suggest in paragraph 5.142, it is my view that Mr Walmsley should have consulted the South Asian Department of the Foreign and Commonwealth Office in 1998. As he did not, it is difficult to speculate whether or not any information which he might have been given would have influenced the outcome of the naturalisation.

5.218 Otherwise, I am satisfied with Mr Walmsley's decision making in relation to Mr S P Hinduja, although I have set out in this chapter some of my concerns about aspects of the way in which the case was handled. In particular, the paucity of minutes on the case file has not made it possible for me to establish an audit trail to verify why Mr Walmsley came to the decisions he did. However, he has given me explanations for the decisions which he took which I find acceptable.

5.219. I am satisfied by the reasons given for Mr S P Hinduja's case being granted priority and accept that there are reasonable grounds to argue that the 819 days he had spent out of the country should not have prevented him from being granted citizenship.

5.220. I am satisfied that Mr Walmsley was not influenced in his decision making by any contacts which he may have had with the Hinduja brothers or by anyone else who made representations or enquiries on his behalf.

CHAPTER 6

PRAKASH HINDUJA

6.1. I have already explained in Chapter 1, paragraph 1.2, why I have decided also to investigate the approaches made to the Home Office in relation to Mr Prakash (also known as "PP") Hinduja's interest in naturalisation, in so far as they are relevant to my review of Mr S P Hinduja's naturalisation application.

Background

6.2. The first time when Mr Prakash Hinduja comes into the picture, as far as this Review is concerned, is when Mr Mandelson handed a letter to Mr Straw in May 2000. The letter in question was written by Mr G P Hinduja (attached at Annex S) and asked Mr Mandelson's advice on whether the Home Office were likely to approach a citizenship application from Prakash in a positive way. Mr G P Hinduja anticipated potential problems. Mr Prakash Hinduja would need to become a permanent resident of the UK and would also need to meet the residence requirement in terms of spending more time in the United Kingdom. But Mr G P Hinduja concluded that:

> "the benefits he would bring as a UK citizen would far outweigh any hurdles that there may be.".

6.3. Mr Mandelson did not recall how he received Mr G P Hinduja's letter of 18 May 2000. He thought that he might have been given it at a meeting with Mr G P Hinduja, or it might have been sent to him by post. Mr Mandelson said that he then passed the letter on to Mr Straw, as Home Secretary, without comment. Mr Straw thought that he had been asked to sort the matter out quickly, although this might have been a reference to giving Mr G P Hinduja a prompt reply to his letter rather than any priority if he, Prakash Hinduja, provided any future application for citizenship. Mr Mandelson appears to have handled this letter entirely properly, in that he passed it to the Home Office to consider without further comment.

6.4. I have been unable to establish how exactly the letter passed from Mr Mandelson to Mr Straw. But this is not an issue of any significance.

6.5. On receipt of the letter, Mr Straw wrote a manuscript note on his copy to the private secretary in his private office who dealt with immigration and nationality issues, Dr Mara Goldstein. Mr Straw's manuscript note said:

> "Mara—Mr Mandelson raised this matter with me. Please have a word first then get some advice.".

Mr Straw had written underneath this:

> "? Zola Budd"

a comment which he had circled. Mr Straw does not appear to have discussed this reference to Ms Budd with Dr Goldstein. When I met him, Mr Straw recalled that there had been some attention focussed on Ms Budd, an athlete, when she was granted British citizenship under the previous Government, but he could not recall why he had referred to her in this way on the top of Mr G P Hinduja's letter. I do not regard this as significant.

6.6. Dr Goldstein told me that Mr Straw passed her the letter from Mr G P Hinduja on 25 May 2000. Mr Straw had asked her whether she knew who the Hindujas were. Dr Goldstein had said that she did not. She told me that Mr Straw said that the Hindujas brought a lot of business into the United Kingdom and that the letter from Mr G P Hinduja should be considered by the Home Office in that context.

6.7. Having given Mr G P Hinduja's letter to his office, Mr Straw wrote Mr Mandelson a hand-written acknowledgement on 25 May 2000 (Annex T). This said that he was:

> "following the matter up personally and will be back in touch as soon as I can."

The letter was marked "Personal". Mr Straw said that it was his usual practice to write personal acknowledgements in this way when he received letters from close colleagues. Ms Hilary Jackson, his principal private secretary, confirmed this and said that it was also Mr Straw's usual practice to take a copy of these hand-written letters so that they could be placed on the file in the Home Office. Mr Mandelson said that he was slightly surprised by the personal note from Mr Straw, but thought that this was consistent with Mr Straw's normal practice. Mr Mandelson's view was that Mr Straw was a considerate Minister who liked to deal with colleagues in a courteous way. He did not think that there was anything improper about the fact that Mr Straw had written him a manuscript acknowledgement in this way.

6.8, I agree with this interpretation. Mr Mandelson was a high profile and senior Government colleague and Mr Straw would have wanted to demonstrate to Mr Mandelson, as he would other such colleagues, that the matter which he had raised with Mr Straw was being dealt with efficiently and properly.

6.9. Mr Goldstein e-mailed Mr Walmsley in the Nationality Directorate in Liverpool on 25 May 2000 to ask him to telephone her so that they could discuss the letter from Mr G P Hinduja. She had sent it to him on the same day asking him to:

> "look at this request and provide advice as soon as possible and certainly by 15 June".

On the typed covering sheet which accompanied Mr G P Hinduja's letter, Dr Goldstein had described the subject of the letter as:

> "British citizenship request of Prakash Hinduja. Letter from Mr Mandelson to Home Secretary, 18 May".

When we met her on 31 January, Dr Goldstein explained that this was an error and that, in fact, there had been no letter from Mr Mandelson, just the one from Mr G P Hinduja.

6.10. Since she had not heard from Mr Walmsley, Dr Goldstein telephoned him on 31 May 2000 and spoke to one of Mr Walmsley's colleagues, Mr Tony Dalton. Mr Dalton took a message which he passed on to Mr Walmsley by e-mail. This e-mail message to Mr Walmsley said:

> "Mara Goldstein telephoned me today because she was unable to contact you.
>
> She said she had faxed you details of a request made to the Home Secretary in a letter dated 18 May on behalf of Prakash Hinduja. This is a sensitive case because of the prominence of the family. They have all been granted British citizenship except for Prakash Hinduja who is resident in Switzerland and visits the UK periodically. The family have considerable business interests which can bring benefit to UK interests. The Home Secretary would like the case to be dealt with "helpfully".
>
> Mara asked me to pass this message on to you—she is concerned that the case should be dealt with quickly.".

6.11. I was particularly interested to know what Dr Goldstein understood by the phrase:

> "the Home Secretary would like the case to be dealt with "helpfully"

and whether this indicated that the Home Secretary wanted Mr Prakash Hinduja to be given any form of priority or special treatment. Dr Goldstein said that she thought that Mr Straw's attitude to this case had been that, as the Hindujas brought certain benefits to the United Kingdom, he would want the Home Office to do what it could, within the rules, to grant naturalisation. Dr Goldstein said that this was not an unusual way for Mr Straw to approach such a case. She thought that if Mr Straw thought that he had come across a deserving case then he was in favour of officials using their discretion to decide in favour of the applicant, as long as that would be within the rules.

6.12. Mr Straw confirmed this interpretation. He said that, in his view, the word "helpfully" meant that he wanted the matter dealt with properly, as was his approach to all cases, but that if it was right, within the rules, to exercise discretion in this case, then the Home Office should look to do so. Mr Straw said that he had not been proposing that Prakash Hinduja should be given citizenship just because he might bring benefits to the country. He had not wanted officials to depart, in any way, from the usual rules or processes for granting nationality. In sum, he had wanted them to approach

Mr G P Hinduja's letter sympathetically, but strictly within the rules. Mr Walmsley put a similar interpretation on the word "helpfully". Mr Dalton said that Dr Goldstein had not explained to him what she had meant by "helpfully" as this had not arisen in the conversation.

6.13. Having heard these accounts, I am satisfied that the use of the word "helpfully" did not have any suspicious connotations, nor did it suggest that the Home Secretary wished to give Mr Prakash Hinduja any preferential treatment which he would not have offered in other cases of this kind. During my interview with him on 31 January, Mr Straw said that he had, also, recently, been asked to deal with the nationality cases of two international musicians. He thought that both of these musicians were deserving and would benefit the United Kingdom if they became citizens. He therefore had asked for their cases to be considered in much the same way as he had suggested in the case of Mr Prakash Hinduja. I am also satisfied that, at no time, did Mr Straw suggest that officials should consider the enquiry from Mr G P Hinduja in any way which was outside the usual nationality rules or processes.

6.14. I also asked Dr Goldstein why she had asked for advice from Mr Walmsley:

"as soon as possible, and certainly by 15 June"

and whether this was an indication that Mr Prakash Hinduja was being given priority. Dr Goldstein said that giving officials this amount of time to provide advice to the Home Secretary (in this case, one month after the date of Mr G P Hinduja's letter; 21 days from receipt of the letter) was her usual practice. It did not represent preferential treatment.

6.15. Dr Goldstein said that she had asked for the papers to be brought forward on 15 June and telephoned Mr Walmsley on that date to chase up the response to Mr Hinduja's letter. Again, Dr Goldstein said this was her usual practice. This was corroborated by Ms Jackson, who confirmed that Dr Goldstein had a very effective "Bring Forward" system and would speak to officials if advice had not been received by the date it had been requested.

6.16. Mr Walmsley's advice arrived on 22 June 2000, in the form of a submission to the Home Secretary (Annex U). Unlike his submission of 14 August 1998 in relation to Mr S P Hinduja, this submission was copied to the Immigration Minister, the Permanent Secretary and others in the usual way. Mr Walmsley's submission concluded that "on the face of it" it was unlikely that Mr Prakash Hinduja, who at the time lived in Switzerland, would meet the requirements that he should have indefinite leave to remain in the United Kingdom. Attached to the submission was a draft letter for Mr Straw to send to Mr Mandelson, which reported this advice. This letter, with some drafting amendments, but none of substance, was sent on 26 June 2000 (Annex V). At the end of the letter, Mr Straw had added a manuscript note:

"I hope this is helpful. I'd be happy to have a further word with you.".

6.17. Dr Goldstein had annotated the submission:

> "You asked for a positive approach. Seems you do have discretion, but Andrew proposes he discusses with the solicitor first. Content with this approach for now and ask AW to report back to you in 1 month?".

6.18. Mr Straw ticked and initialled the submission.

6.19. The letter of 26 June 2000 to Mr Mandelson had suggested that Mr Walmsley would contact Mr Hinduja's solicitors to:

> "offer advice on how he might obtain settlement under the immigration rules and on the timing of any application for citizenship." .

Although Dr Goldstein had changed Mr Walmsley's draft letter to make the tone friendlier, this part of the letter was not changed. Having spoken to Mr Walmsley about this, I am satisfied that the suggestion that he would contact the solicitors did not indicate any preferential treatment for Mr Hinduja, but was an example of Mr Walmsley trying to provide a helpful service to applicants and their representatives. Following his involvement with the cases of Mr GP and Mr SP Hinduja, Mr Walmsley said that he would have previously had a number of dealings with the Hindujas' solicitor, Mr Richard Hoare, previously. Mr Straw said that, on reading the draft letter, he had wondered whether it was usual practice for an official to approach the solicitors direct, but thought that if Mr Walmsley was willing to initiate contact with the solicitors, so be it.

6.20. Mr Mandelson told me that, on receipt of the letter of 26 June 2000 from Mr Straw, he would have copied the letter to Mr G P Hinduja in the normal way. He confirmed that he had had no further contact with the Home Office about Mr Prakash Hinduja's naturalisation and did not know what had happened in relation to it following his contact with the Home Secretary. I have found no evidence to contradict this.

6.21. Meanwhile, back in the Home Office, Dr Goldstein chased up a progress report at the end of August 2000, but was told that Mr Prakash Hinduja's legal advisers were in no hurry to take forward his application for naturalisation. She therefore let matters lie.

Findings

6.22. I do not believe that there is anything suspicious about Mr Straw's hand-written letter of 25 May 2000; the use of the words "helpfully" or "positive" in respect of Mr Prakash Hinduja's interest in naturalisation; the efficiency with which Dr Goldstein chased a response from officials; or Mr Walmsley's suggestion that he contact the solicitors direct.

6.23. I am satisfied that Mr G P Hinduja's letter of 18 May 2000 was dealt with entirely properly by Mr Mandelson, Mr Straw and his office and the Nationality Directorate in the Home Office.

CHAPTER 7

KEITH VAZ MP

7.1. Because of the prominence which Mr Vaz has received in connection with the subject matter of this review, it is, I believe, appropriate, and also fair to him, to describe his role in the history of the applications for naturalisation by the Hinduja brothers and to put it in the context of the position which he holds in the Asian community in this country. I have interviewed Mr Vaz and he has supplied me with a file of his correspondence. Some of it is contained in the files of the Nationality Directorate. I think that it is right to place on record my impression that he has been open and frank in the way in which he has approached my Review and has willingly provided me with all the information which I have sought.

7.2. Mr Vaz was first elected as a Member of Parliament in 1987. He was the first Asian Member of Parliament since 1922 and until 1992 was the only Asian Member. As such, he became (to use his own words) something of a magnet to members of the Asian community, who looked on him to represent their interests, whether or not they happened to be his constituents. In the nature of things, he became actively involved in issues which concerned the community such as race relations, immigration and nationality. In this role he attended a large number of community events, although he has, necessarily, had to reduce his attendance since becoming a Minister. He has about 35,000 Asians in his Leicester East constituency and is expected to visit parts of India such as Gujarat. As well as being a well-known figure in India, he has, effectively, acquired a national constituency in this country.

7.3. One of the issues which has attracted comment is the fact that Mr Vaz has, on occasions, taken up cases on behalf of members of the Asian community who are not his constituents. He has explained to me that, where possible, he has referred those who have approached him and who are not his constituents to their constituency MP, but there were some occasions when it was quicker and easier for him to deal with the matter and others when they preferred him to represent their interests.

7.4. Mr Vaz said that he had met the Hinduja brothers at many functions. Because of their position as leading and wealthy members of the Asian community in this country, most important events involving members of the community were attended by them and some of these were hosted by the Hindujas. It is clear that many prominent politicians of all parties had attended functions hosted by them or at which they were present. Mr Vaz said that he had got to know them very well.

7.5. Mr Vaz said that he had also been involved in supporting Millennium projects proposed by organisations and members of the Asian community. One of these had been a project called Concordia, a project with a religious theme, proposed by the Hindujas, in Peterborough, which he had, in common with other Asian projects, supported. This project was rejected by the Millennium Commission so it was proposed in 1997 to attempt to get the project accepted for the Dome. On 17 July 1997 Mr Vaz wrote to Mr Mandelson, at the request of the Hindujas, saying that he was disappointed that there were no Asian projects in the Dome and saying that he hoped that it might be accepted for the Dome (see also Chapter 8, paragraph 8.2). Having described Mr Vaz's role in representing the Asian community, I now turn to the handling of the naturalisation applications from the Hinduja brothers. To some extent I have touched on the contacts which Mr Vaz had with the Home Office over these applications in Chapters 4 and 5.

7.6. The first recorded contact between Mr Vaz and the Home Office over the applications for naturalisation from Mr G P Hinduja and Mr S P Hinduja was in December 1993, when Mr Vaz wrote to Mr Charles Wardle MP, the then Minister in charge of immigration and nationality matters, (that is to say after the applications had been refused in 1991). Mr Vaz's letter is not on the file, but Mr Wardle's reply is. He was clearly asked about the scope for exercising discretion to waive excess absences. Mr Wardle said that he could not give any guarantees about how the discretion would be exercised in a particular case, as much depended on individual circumstances, and advised that new applications should be sent and should be carefully timed (presumably because of the requirement to be in the United Kingdom at the start of the five year period). They should be sent direct to Mr Walmsley, the Head of the then Nationality Division. During 1994, there was further correspondence from Mr Vaz to Mr Walmsley, enquiring about progress.

7.7. On 23 December 1994 Mr Walmsley wrote to Mr Vaz requesting details about Mr S P Hinduja's absences from the United Kingdom over the past five years and confirmation from the tax authorities that he was resident in the United Kingdom for tax purposes. In February 1997, Mr Vaz wrote again, enquiring about progress about the applications from both brothers (but without supplying any details). In March 1997 Mr Walmsley replied giving the up-to-date position. Mr Walmsley's submission of 3 July 1997 recommending that Mr G P Hinduja be granted naturalisation (see Chapter 4 above) mentioned that the matter had been raised orally by Mr Vaz with Mr O'Brien, although there is no record of when that took place. The next letter on the file from Mr Vaz is one of 15 October 1998 recording a telephone conversation with Mr Walmsley about Mr S P Hinduja's case and thanking him for his help in resolving the issue. This appears to be Mr Vaz's last intervention in the matter.

7.8. I have dealt at some length with Mr Vaz's role in the applications for naturalisation by the Hinduja brothers because of the comments which this has excited. It is clear that he made representations and enquiries on behalf of the brothers, particularly Mr G P Hinduja. He also made representations on behalf of many others, both individuals and organisations, in connection with immigration and nationality matters. It is also clear that a number of other prominent public figures made representations on behalf of the Hinduja brothers. Some of these are mentioned in earlier chapters. It is true that Mr Vaz was probably more vigorous in his representative role than most of the other people who made representations. But I believe that it is legitimate to view Mr Vaz's role in the context of his unique position in the Asian community, which I have already described. I have been able to find nothing improper in his relations with the Home Office over these matters. Mr Walmsley has told me that he did not feel that he was put under any improper pressure from Mr Vaz or that Mr Vaz's interest in assisting the Hindujas was unduly close. Mr Vaz has said that there was never any suggestion from the Hinduja brothers that there was or should be a link between their sponsorship of the Dome and their efforts to obtain naturalisation (see Chapter 8 on the Dome). Indeed, Mr Vaz has told me that he never took part in any discussions about sponsoring any part of the Dome.

7.9. When Mr Vaz first became involved with making representations on behalf of the Hinduja brothers, he was, of course, a Backbench Member of Parliament. He continued to enquire about their cases after he became the Parliamentary Private Secretary to the Law Officers. Given the history of his interest in the naturalisation applications and Mr Vaz's position in the Asian community, I do not think that there is any reason to criticise Mr Vaz on that score.

7.10. It has been suggested that Mr Vaz wrote to the Prime Minister and Mr Mandelson about the Hinduja brothers' applications. There is no trace of any such letter in the Prime Minister's Office or elsewhere. Mr Vaz categorically denied this suggestion and said that it would have been absurd to do so, as it would have achieved nothing. Given that Mr Vaz had regular contacts with the Home Office over immigration and nationality matters and how well he knew how the system worked, I find the suggestion difficult to credit and I accept Mr Vaz's explanation.

7.11. There have been stories in the press about "topping and tailing" letters drafted by the Hinduja brothers. Mr Vaz explained that, if this had happened (and he has no record of it), it might have been dealt with by one of his staff in connection with the Concordia project and not himself. This has been borne out by Mr Vaz's explanation that a letter of 30 October 1997 from him to Darin Jewell—former assistant to the Hindujas—was dealt with by his constituency office. This letter has been signed by way of a rubber stamp facsimile of Mr Vaz's signature rather than Mr Vaz signing it personally. I do not regard this as a matter of any great significance.

7.12. Finally, I will deal with an allegation I became aware of that Mr Vaz had attended a meeting at New Zealand House, the business premises of the Hinduja brothers, where he had discussed issues concerning their possible extradition to India to face the investigation which was being carried out into the Bofors scandal. The article alleged that Mr Vaz had passed secrets to the Hindujas. Mr Vaz categorically denied that he would have discussed this issue at any meeting with the Hinduja brothers or that he had any priviledged information to pass on. If they had raised the issue, he would have referred them to the FCO Minister responsible for the relevant matters. There was a meeting in the FCO at the request of Mr Barry Gardiner MP in January 2001 to discuss the issue of extradition and their status as British citizens. The Minister present was Baroness Scotland. Mr Vaz did not attend that meeting. There was also a letter from Mr Piara Khabra MP of 15 December 2000 to Rt Hon Robin Cook MP asking for support for the Hinduja brothers. Mr Vaz was not involved in drafting the reply to this letter, but he had seen a copy of it. The reply, signed by Mr Cook, said that both the Hinduja brothers would get the full consular support available to any British citizen, but there could be no question of intervening in the due legal process in India.

CHAPTER 8

SPONSORSHIP OF DOME

8.1. I have already described in Chapter 7, the part which Mr Vaz played in supporting Millennium projects proposed by members of the Asian community, including the Hinduja brothers and which, in their case, became a Dome project. As I have already said in the Introduction to my Report, I am only concerned with issues related to the sponsorship of the Dome by the Hinduja brothers, insofar as it is necessary to do so for the purpose of establishing whether there was any link between their offers of sponsorship and their attempts to obtain British citizenship.

8.2. I begin the story at the point when the present Government arrived in Office. In June and July 1997 there was correspondence between the Hinduja brothers and Mr Mandelson about prospects for obtaining the approval of the Millennium Commission to the funding of the Concordia project. This was a project for the establishment of a multi-ethnic cultural centre near Peterborough. Mr Mandelson, who, as Minister Without Portfolio at the Cabinet Office was responsible for the Dome, whilst politely wishing them well, said it was for the Commission to decide on the merits of competing bids. On 17 July 1997 Mr Vaz wrote to Mr Mandelson, suggesting that the Concordia project, put forward by the Hinduja brothers, had not attracted the approval of the Millennium Commission and asking that it be considered as part of the projects for the Dome. In the same letter, Mr Vaz drew attention to the lack of funding for other "Asian-led projects" pointing out that these projects had received only £5m of the £900m allocated by the Commission. Mr Mandelson replied on 11 August 1997 saying that the project was still under consideration by the Millennium Commission. As far as the Dome was concerned, he said that consideration of what should be incorporated into the Dome was a matter for the New Millennium Experience Company and he had no direct control over the content. He suggested that Mr Vaz should write to Miss Jennie Page, the Chief Executive of the Company. In February 1998 Mr S P Hinduja wrote to the Prime Minister and Mr Mandelson offering to contribute to the Dome. There is no record that the Prime Minister replied to that letter. There was then contact between Miss Page and the Hinduja brothers. On 6 October 1998 Mr S P Hinduja wrote to Mr Mandelson asking for his assistance in resolving difficulties which had arisen over conditions attached to their offer of sponsorship of what was then called the Spirit Zone of the Dome. By this time they had offered to underwrite the Zone in the sum of £3 million. There is no record on the files of any reply to this letter.

8.3. On 19 October 1998 Miss Page wrote to the Department of Culture, Media and Sport, the Department responsible for handling issues relating to the Dome, asking that formal checks should be instituted within Government about the Hinduja group of companies. It was normal procedure for the Millennium

Experience Company to check on the status, credit and general standing of potential sponsors. In the case of the Hinduja companies, it was not easy to be clear about the full extent of involvement between them and the Government, because of the diverse nature of their business. There were also concerns within Government about reports about their business background.

8.4. On 3 November 1998 a submission was put forward to Mr Mandelson, who was, by this time, the Secretary of State for Trade and Industry, but who had retained responsibility for the Dome. This minute was accompanied by an account of the intelligence material which I have already described in Chapter 5. The minute stated that although there were a number of allegations of improper, and in some cases criminal, behaviour, none of it was conclusive. There was a risk of adverse publicity if any of the various proceedings or investigations currently under way abroad were to become public, but, on balance, the risk was worth taking. It recommended that Miss Page be advised that there was no reason for her not to continue negotiations with the Hinduja brothers. Mr Mandelson minuted this submission in the following terms:

> "I agree that they are an above average risk but without firm evidence of wrongdoing how could we bar them from involvement in sponsorship? We are right to reduce our exposure to them. I wonder how this involvement got publicity in the first place. Incidentally, if Mr S P Hinduja wishes to pursue his citizenship application he can do so without further involvement or commendation from me!".

In view of reports which have appeared in the media, I think that I should say that it is possible that Mr Mandelson saw some intelligence material before 3 November 1998, but I am satisfied that this could not have been before 21 October 1998.

8.5. Mr Mandelson has said to me that he regards this comment as consistent with his position throughout and that at no stage did he seek to advance the applications for naturalisation made by any of the Hinduja brothers. I have found no evidence to the contrary and I accept Mr Mandelson's explanation. As regards the decision to allow negotiations over the Dome funding to continue, this was a judgment which Mr Mandelson came to after receiving advice from his officials. He followed their advice and, again, I find no grounds to criticise him on that score.

8.6. There is one further issue concerning Mr Mandelson's contacts with the Hinduja brothers. An article in The Mirror on 25 January 2001 reported that at a meeting in August 1988 at the headquarters of the Hinduja companies in New Zealand House, Mr Darin Jewell alleged that naturalisation was discussed. It was also alleged that Mr Mandelson attended this meeting. Mr Mandelson has said that he has no knowledge of any such meeting if there was one and, if naturalisation was discussed, it was for the purposes of the Hindujas and not shared with Mr Mandelson. I can find no record of any such meeting on the official papers and I have not considered it necessary to contact Mr Jewell. I accept Mr Mandelson's explanation.

8.7. I must deal with one other matter concerning the sponsorship of the Dome. An article appeared in the Daily Telegraph on 1 February this year suggesting that Lord Levy brokered a deal with the Hinduja brothers to sponsor the Dome. Hon Nicholas Soames MP, wrote to me asking me to investigate this report. I have spoken to Lord Levy. He told me that Mr Mandelson had contacted him to say that he was concerned about the arrangements for the sponsorship of the Dome and a meeting was held in the Department of Trade and Industry on 23 October 1998 between him, Mr Mandelson, Miss Page and officials. There was a later meeting on 29 October 1998 in the House of Lords, at which Lord Levy and two of the Hinduja brothers were present. Mr Mandelson did not attend this meeting. At that meeting Lord Levy said that a gift would be more satisfactory instead of the previous "underwriting" arrangement which was suggested and a gift of £1 million was offered instead. Lord Levy said to me that, at no time, was there, at this meeting, any reference, explicit or implicit, to the obtaining of passports or citizenship by the Hindujas. I accept his explanation.

8.8. I have also asked Miss Page whether, in her dealings with the Hinduja brothers, any such reference was ever made and she has confirmed that there was no such reference. Again, I have no reason to doubt the accuracy of what she has said.

8.9. I will now sum up the account which I have given of the handling of relations with the Hinduja brothers over the funding of first, the Concordia project, and then the Spirit Zone of the Dome.

8.10. It is clear that they wished the Government and, in particular, Mr Mandelson, as the Minister responsible for the Dome, to accept their ideas for ethnic representation in the Dome project in return for offers of sponsorship. Although Ministers gave their approaches general encouragement, the detailed negotiations were carried out by Miss Page, as Chief Executive of the New Millennium Experience Company. Ministers generally and Mr Mandelson, in particular, acted correctly. The judgment which Mr Mandelson reached to allow negotiations with the Hindujas to continue, notwithstanding the intelligence information, was in accordance with official advice and was a reasonable one in the circumstances. As a matter of timing, discussions with the Hindujas over sponsorship were being carried out over the same period as their efforts to obtain citizenship. But I have found no evidence either that they sought to link these discussions to their desire to obtain citizenship or that any Minister, whether Mr Mandelson, Mr Vaz, or anyone else, sought at any time to make such a connection.

CHAPTER 9

PRIVATE OFFICE WORKING PRACTICES

9.1. Throughout this Review, I have been hampered by the lack of consistent record keeping in the private offices which were involved in the events which I have described, that is to say, in particular, Mr O'Brien's private office in the Home Office and Mr Mandelson's private office in the Cabinet Office, when he was Minister Without Portfolio. The account of the events in June or July 1998 when Mr Mandelson or his office were contacting Mr O'Brien's office over Mr S P Hinduja's naturalisation query is based solely on the recollections of those involved, two and a half years after the events, unaided by documentary evidence. (The e-mail of 2 July 1998 does not really assist in describing what happened.) Memories are necessarily hazy and it is not surprising if there are inconsistencies in peoples' recollections. The accounts of the contacts between Mr Mandelson's office in Belfast and Mr Straw's office in London in December 2000 and January 2001 are better recorded and, of course, those events are much more recent. Even so recollections differ amongst the participants.

9.2. If the telephone calls in June or July 1998 had been recorded in writing and there had been a more consistent practice of monitoring telephone conversations of Ministers and recording their content, it might have been possible for more definite conclusions to have been reached about what was said by whom to whom and about the sequence of events.

9.3. I recognise that the pace of life in a Minister's office is extremely hectic and, with the best will in the world, it is very difficult for private secretaries to find the time to record in writing the content of telephone conversations and, invariably, to monitor their Ministers' conversations. It is also not easy, in advance, to spot what is important enough to monitor and what is purely ephemeral or of trivial significance. But the events which I have reviewed show that what may seem trivial at the time may, later, attract a much greater importance, as has now happened. I would not wish anything which I have said in this Chapter or elsewhere in the Report to be construed as criticism of any of the private secretaries involved, who were, I believe, under great pressure (as are nearly all private secretaries) and were doing their best in difficult circumstances.

9.4. Nevertheless, I recommend that Departments review the working practices in their private offices with a view to seeing whether there should be more regular monitoring of telephone conversations between Ministers and better written records of telephone calls between offices. Such a review might extend to record keeping generally e.g. of minutes issuing from and received by private offices, and might take into account the impact on record keeping of the widespread introduction of electronic communications, such as e-mail. I recognise that a balance has to be struck here, in a world of finite resources. But if resources need to be increased, the case for doing so should be seriously examined.

SIR ANTHONY HAMMOND KCB QC
8th March 2001

ANNEXES

ANNEXES

ANNEX A

Mr. Straw: My right hon. Friend the Prime Minister announced on 24 January that he had asked former Treasury Solicitor, Sir Anthony Hammond QC, to review the full circumstances surrounding approaches to the Home Office in connection with the possibility of an application for naturalisation by Mr. S. P. Hinduja in 1998. Sir Anthony started his review on Thursday 25 January. After an initial reading of the papers, Sir Anthony has decided that, in order to fulfil the terms of reference of his review of the application for naturalisation of S. P. Hinduja, it is appropriate for him to look at the circumstances of the granting of naturalisation in respect of G. P. Hinduja because the circumstances of both applications are closely related. For the same reason, he has also decided that it is appropriate for him to look at the circumstances surrounding the inquiries about naturalisation in respect of Prakesh Hinduja.

Sir Anthony aims to complete his review as quickly as possible, consistently with the need to conduct a thorough investigation. I understand that on the information currently available to Sir Anthony, he hopes to complete the review by the end of February. The report will be published and copies will be placed in the Vote Office and the Library. It would be inappropriate for me to pre-empt the outcome of this review.

Annex B

Those I interviewed:

Mr Richard Abel	principal private secretary to Sir Richard Wilson
Mr Lee Bailey	private secretary to Mr O'Brien 2000/2001
Mr Norman Baker MP	Member of Parliament for Lewes
Mr David Barnes	assistant private secretary to Mr O'Brien 1998
Mr Mick Cain	Integrated Casework Directorate, Immigration & Nationality Directorate
Mr Alastair Campbell	Prime Minister's official spokesman
Mrs Lyndsey Curtis	diary secretary to Mr O'Brien 1998
Mr Tony Dalton	Integrated Casework Directorate, Immigration & Nationality Directorate
Ms Maria Daniels	diary secretary to Mr Mandelson in the Cabinet Office 1998
Mr Patrick Diamond	special adviser to Mr Mandelson 2001
Ms Rosemary Earp	Integrated Casework Directorate, Immigration & Nationality Directorate
Mr John Fiennes	private secretary to Mr Mandelson in the DTI 1998
Ms Jane Fowler	assistant private secretary to Mr Straw 2000/2001
Dr Mara Goldstein	private secretary to Mr Straw 2000/2001
Ms Angela Hines	Integrated Casework Directorate, Immigration & Nationality Directorate
Ms Cathy Hume	private secretary to Mrs Roche 2000/2001
Mr Doug Hunt	Integrated Casework Directorate, Immigration & Nationality Directorate
Mr Rupert Huxter	principal private secretary to Mr Mandelson in the Cabinet Office 1998
Ms Hilary Jackson	principal private secretary to Mr Straw 2000/2001
Ms Bharti Jaycee	member of staff in Mr Vaz's constituency office
Mr Mark Langdale	principal private secretary to Mr Mandelson in the Cabinet Office 1998
Mr Andrew Lansley MP	Shadow Cabinet Office Minister
Mr Matthew Laxton	assistant private secretary to Mr O'Brien 1998
Lord Levy	
The Rt. Hon Peter Mandelson MP	Member of Parliament for Hartlepool
Ms Kirsten McFarlane	private secretary to Mr Mandelson in the Northern Ireland Office 2000/2001
Mr James Morrison	private secretary to Mr Vaz in the Foreign & Commonwealth Office 2001
Ms Jacky Moore	Integrated Casework Directorate, Immigration & Nationality Directorate
Miss Bryony Morris	assistant private secretary to Mr O'Brien 1998
Mr Mike O'Brien MP	Parliamentary Under Secretary of State, Home Office

Mr Keith Oliver	Integrated Casework Directorate, Immigration & Nationality Directorate
Mr Jon Payne	private secretary to Mr O'Brien 1998
Mr Jonathan Powell	Prime Minister's Chief of Staff
Mr A R Rawsthorne	formerly Immigration & Nationality Directorate
Mrs Barbara Roche MP	Minister of State, Home Office
Ms Veronica Sanders	Integrated Casework Directorate, Immigration & Nationality Directorate
Ms Emma Scott	assistant private secretary to Mr Mandelson in the Cabinet Office 1998
The Rt. Hon Jack Straw MP	Home Secretary
Ms Clare Sumner	private secretary to the Prime Minister
Ms Sarah Todd	private secretary to Mr Mandelson in the Northern Ireland Office 2000-2001
Mr Andrew Tyrie MP	Member of Parliament for Chichester
Mr Varum Uberoi	assistant private secretary to Mr O' Brien 2000/2001
Mr Alan Underwood	Head of Integrated Casework Directorate
Mr Keith Vaz MP	Minister of State, Foreign & Commonwealth Office
Mr Charles Wardle MP	Member of Parliament for Bexhill and Battle
Mr Andrew Warmsley	Integrated Casework Directorate, Immigration & Nationality Directorate
The Rt. Hon Ann Widdecombe MP	Shadow Home Secretary
Sir Richard Wilson GCB	Secretary of the Cabinet
Ms Deirdre Wright	Integrated Casework Directorate, Immigration & Nationality Directorate

Departments and individuals who supplied me with information:

Miss Jennie Page	formerly Chief Executive of the New Millennium Experience Company

Cabinet Office
Department of Culture Media and Sport
Foreign & Commonwealth Office
Government Communication Headquarters
Home Office
Northern Ireland Office
Secret Intelligence Service
Security Service

ANNEX C

1534   c. **61**   *British Nationality Act 1981*

PART I

(6) Subsection (5) applies to—

(*a*) Crown service under the government of a dependent territory ; and

(*b*) paid or unpaid service (not falling within paragraph (*a*)) as a member of any body established by law in a dependent territory members of which are appointed by or on behalf of the Crown.

Acquisition by registration: nationals for purposes of the Community Treaties.

5. A British Dependent Territories citizen who falls to be treated as a national of the United Kingdom for the purposes of the Community Treaties shall be entitled to be registered as a British citizen if an application is made for his registration as such a citizen.

Acquisition by naturalisation.

6.—(1) If, on an application for naturalisation as a British citizen made by a person of full age and capacity, the Secretary of State is satisfied that the applicant fulfils the requirements of Schedule 1 for naturalisation as such a citizen under this subsection, he may, if he thinks fit, grant to him a certificate of naturalisation as such a citizen.

(2) If, on an application for naturalisation as a British citizen made by a person of full age and capacity who on the date of the application is married to a British citizen, the Secretary of State is satisfied that the applicant fulfils the requirements of Schedule 1 for naturalisation as such a citizen under this subsection, he may, if he thinks fit, grant to him a certificate of naturalisation as such a citizen.

Acquisition after commencement : special cases

Right to registration by virtue of residence in U.K. or relevant employment.

1971 c. 77.

7.—(1) A person shall be entitled, on an application for his registration as a British citizen made (subject to subsections (6) and (7)) within five years after commencement, to be registered as such a citizen if either of the following requirements is satisfied in his case, namely—

(*a*) that, if paragraphs 2 and 3 (but not paragraph 4 or 5) of Schedule 1 to the Immigration Act 1971 had remained in force, he would (had he applied for it) have been, on the date of the application under this subsection, entitled under the said paragraph 2 to be registered in the United Kingdom as a citizen of the United Kingdom and Colonies ; or

(*b*) that, if section 5A of the 1948 Act (and section 2 of the Immigration Act 1971 as in force immediately before commencement) had remained in force, he would (had he applied for it) have been, both at commencement and on the date of the application under this subsection, entitled under section 5A(1) of the 1948 Act to

1578   c. **61**   *British Nationality Act 1981*

SCHEDULES

Sections 6 and 18.

SCHEDULE 1

REQUIREMENTS FOR NATURALISATION

Naturalisation as a British citizen under section 6(1)

1.—(1) Subject to paragraph 2, the requirements for naturalisation as a British citizen under section 6(1) are, in the case of any person who applies for it—

   (*a*) the requirements specified in sub-paragraph (2) of this paragraph, or the alternative requirement specified in sub-paragraph (3) of this paragraph ; and

   (*b*) that he is of good character ; and

   (*c*) that he has a sufficient knowledge of the English, Welsh or Scottish Gaelic language ; and

   (*d*) that either—

      (i) his intentions are such that, in the event of a certificate of naturalisation as a British citizen being granted to him, his home or (if he has more than one) his principal home will be in the United Kingdom ; or

      (ii) he intends, in the event of such a certificate being granted to him, to enter into, or continue in, Crown service under the government of the United Kingdom, or service under an international organisation of which the United Kingdom or Her Majesty's government therein is a member, or service in the employment of a company or association established in the United Kingdom.

(2) The requirements referred to in sub-paragraph (1)(*a*) of this paragraph are—

   (*a*) that the applicant was in the United Kingdom at the beginning of the period of five years ending with the date of the application, and that the number of days on which he was absent from the United Kingdom in that period does not exceed 450 ; and

   (*b*) that the number of days on which he was absent from the United Kingdom in the period of twelve months so ending does not exceed 90 ; and

   (*c*) that he was not at any time in the period of twelve months so ending subject under the immigration laws to any restriction on the period for which he might remain in the United Kingdom ; and

   (*d*) that he was not at any time in the period of five years so ending in the United Kingdom in breach of the immigration laws.

(3) The alternative requirement referred to in sub-paragraph (1)(*a*) of this paragraph is that on the date of the application he is serving outside the United Kingdom in Crown service under the government of the United Kingdom.

Sch. 1

2. If in the special circumstances of any particular case the Secretary of State thinks fit, he may for the purposes of paragraph 1 do all or any of the following things, namely—

　(*a*) treat the applicant as fulfilling the requirement specified in paragraph 1(2)(*a*) or paragraph 1(2)(*b*), or both, although the number of days on which he was absent from the United Kingdom in the period there mentioned exceeds the number there mentioned;

　(*b*) treat the applicant as having been in the United Kingdom for the whole or any part of any period during which he would otherwise fall to be treated under paragraph 9(1) as having been absent;

　(*c*) disregard any such restriction as is mentioned in paragraph 1(2)(*c*), not being a restriction to which the applicant was subject on the date of the application;

　(*d*) treat the applicant as fulfilling the requirement specified in paragraph 1(2)(*d*) although he was in the United Kingdom in breach of the immigration laws in the period there mentioned;

　(*e*) waive the need to fulfil the requirement specified in paragraph 1(1)(*c*) if he considers that because of the applicant's age or physical or mental condition it would be unreasonable to expect him to fulfil it.

Naturalisation as a British citizen under section 6(2)

3. Subject to paragraph 4, the requirements for naturalisation as a British citizen under section 6(2) are, in the case of any person who applies for it—

　(*a*) that he was in the United Kingdom at the beginning of the period of three years ending with the date of the application, and that the number of days on which he was absent from the United Kingdom in that period does not exceed 270; and

　(*b*) that the number of days on which he was absent from the United Kingdom in the period of twelve months so ending does not exceed 90; and

　(*c*) that on the date of the application he was not subject under the immigration laws to any restriction on the period for which he might remain in the United Kingdom; and

　(*d*) that he was not at any time in the period of three years ending with the date of the application in the United Kingdom in breach of the immigration laws; and

　(*e*) the requirement specified in paragraph 1(1)(*b*).

4. Paragraph 2 shall apply in relation to paragraph 3 with the following modifications, namely—

　(*a*) the reference to the purposes of paragraph 1 shall be read as a reference to the purposes of paragraph 3;

　(*b*) the references to paragraphs 1(2)(*a*), 1(2)(*b*) and 1(2)(*d*) shall be read as references to paragaphs 3(*a*), 3(*b*) and 3(*d*) respectively;

P 4

Sᴄʜ. 1   (*c*) paragraph 2(*c*) and (*e*) shall be omitted ; and

(*d*) after paragraph (*e*) there shall be added—

" (*f*) waive the need to fulfil all or any of the requirements specified in paragraph 3(*a*) and (*b*) if on the date
of the application the person to whom the applicant is
married is serving in service to which section 2(1)(*b*)
applies, that person's recruitment for that service having
taken place in the United Kingdom.".

*Naturalisation as a British Dependent Territories citizen under
section 18(1)*

5.—(1) Subject to paragraph 6, the requirements for naturalisation
as a British Dependent Territories citizen under section 18(1) are,
in the case of any person who applies for it—

(*a*) the requirements specified in sub-paragraph (2) of this
paragraph, or the alternative requirement specified in sub-
paragraph (3) of this paragraph ; and

(*b*) that he is of good character ; and

(*c*) that he has a sufficient knowledge of the English language
or any other language recognised for official purposes in
the relevant territory ; and

(*d*) that either—

(i) his intentions are such that, in the event of a certificate of naturalisation as a British Dependent Territories
citizen being granted to him, his home or (if he has more
than one) his principal home will be in the relevant territory ; or

(ii) he intends, in the event of such a certificate being
granted to him, to enter into, or continue in, Crown
service under the government of that territory, or service
under an international organisation of which that territory or the government of that territory is a member, or
service in the employment of a company or association
established in that territory.

(2) The requirements referred to in sub-paragraph (1)(*a*) of this
paragraph are—

(*a*) that he was in the relevant territory at the beginning of the
period of five years ending with the date of the application,
and that the number of days on which he was absent from
that territory in that period does not exceed 450 ; and

(*b*) that the number of days on which he was absent from that
territory in the period of twelve months so ending does not
exceed 90 ; and

(*c*) that he was not at any time in the period of twelve months
so ending subject under the immigration laws to any restriction on the period for which he might remain in that
territory ; and

(*d*) that he was not at any time in the period of five years so
ending in that territory in breach of the immigration laws.

(3) The alternative requirement referred to in sub-paragraph (1)(*a*) of this paragraph is that on the date of the application he is serving outside the relevant territory in Crown service under the government of that territory.

6. If in the special circumstances of any particular case the Secretary of State thinks fit, he may for the purposes of paragraph 5 do all or any of the following things, namely—

   (*a*) treat the applicant as fulfilling the requirement specified in paragraph 5(2)(*a*) or paragraph 5(2)(*b*), or both, although the number of days on which he was absent from the relevant territory in the period there mentioned exceeds the number there mentioned ;

   (*b*) treat the applicant as having been in the relevant territory for the whole or any part of any period during which he would otherwise fall to be treated under paragraph 9(2) as having been absent ;

   (*c*) disregard any such restriction as is mentioned in paragraph 5(2)(*c*), not being a restriction to which the applicant was subject on the date of the application ;

   (*d*) treat the applicant as fulfilling the requirement specified in paragraph 5(2)(*d*) although he was in the relevant territory in breach of the immigration laws in the period there mentioned ;

   (*e*) waive the need to fulfil the requirement specified in paragraph 5(1)(*c*) if he considers that because of the applicant's age or physical or mental condition it would be unreasonable to expect him to fulfil it.

Naturalisation as a British Dependent Territories citizen under section 18(2)

7. Subject to paragraph 8, the requirements for naturalisation as a British Dependent Territories citizen under section 18(2) are, in the case of any person who applies for it—

   (*a*) that he was in the relevant territory at the beginning of the period of three years ending with the date of the application, and that the number of days on which he was absent from that territory in that period does not exceed 270 ; and

   (*b*) that the number of days on which he was absent from that territory in the period of twelve months so ending does not exceed 90 ; and

   (*c*) that on the date of the application he was not subject under the immigration laws to any restriction on the period for which he might remain in that territory ; and

   (*d*) that he was not at any time in the period of three years ending with the date of the application in that territory in breach of the immigration laws ; and

   (*e*) the requirement specified in paragraph 5(1)(*b*).

8. Paragraph 6 shall apply in relation to paragraph 7 with the following modifications, namely—

   (*a*) the reference to the purposes of paragraph 5 shall be read as a reference to the purposes of paragraph 7 ;

1582   c. **61**   *British Nationality Act 1981*

Sch. 1

(b) the references to paragraphs 5(2)(*a*), 5(2)(*b*) and 5(2)(*d*) shall be read as references to paragraphs 7(*a*), 7(*b*) and 7(*d*) respectively ;

(c) paragraph 6(*c*) and (*e*) shall be omitted ; and

(d) afer paragraph (*e*) there shall be added—

" (*f*) waive the need to fulfil all or any of the requirements specified in paragraph 7(*a*) and (*b*) if on the date of the application the person to whom the applicant is married is serving in service to which section 16(1)(*b*) applies, that person's recruitment for that service having taken place in a dependent territory.".

Periods to be treated as periods of absence from U.K. or a dependent territory

9.—(1) For the purposes of this Schedule a person shall (subject to paragraph 2(*b*)) be treated as having been absent from the United Kingdom during any of the following periods, that is to say—

1971 c. 77.

(a) any period when he was in the United Kingdom and either was entitled to an exemption under section 8(3) or (4) of the Immigration Act 1971 (exemptions for diplomatic agents etc. and members of the forces) or was a member of the family and formed part of the household of a person so entitled ;

(b) any period when he was detained—

(i) in any place of detention in the United Kingdom in pursuance of a sentence passed on him by a court in the United Kingdom or elsewhere for any offence ;

1959 c. 72.
1975 c. 21.
1961 c. 15 (N.I.).

(ii) in any hospital in the United Kingdom under a hospital order made under Part V of the Mental Health Act 1959 or section 175 or 376 of the Criminal Procedure (Scotland) Act 1975 or Part III of the Mental Health Act (Northern Ireland) 1961, being an order made in connection with his conviction of an offence ; or

(iii) under any power of detention conferred by the immigration laws of the United Kingdom ;

(c) any period when, being liable to be detained as mentioned in paragraph (*b*)(i) or (ii) of this sub-paragraph, he was unlawfully at large or absent without leave and for that reason liable to be arrested or taken into custody ;

(d) any period when, his actual detention under any such power as is mentioned in paragraph (*b*)(iii) of this sub-paragraph being required or specifically authorised, he was unlawfully at large and for that reason liable to be arrested.

(2) For the purposes of this Schedule a person shall (subject to paragraph 6(*b*)) be treated as having been absent from any particular dependent territory during any of the following periods, that is to say—

(a) any period when he was in that territory and either was entitled to an exemption under the immigration laws of that territory corresponding to any such exemption as is mentioned in sub-paragraph (1)(*a*) or was a member of the family and formed part of the household of a person so entitled ;

Sch. 1

(*b*) any period when he was detained—

(i) in any place of detention in the relevant territory in pursuance of a sentence passed on him by a court in that territory or elsewhere for any offence ;

(ii) in any hospital in that territory under a direction (however described) made under any law for purposes similar to Part V of the Mental Health Act 1959 which was for the time being in force in that territory, being a direction made in connection with his conviction of an offence and corresponding to a hospital order under that Part ; or

1959 c. 72.

(iii) under any power of detention conferred by the immigration laws of that territory ;

(*c*) any period when, being liable to be detained as mentioned in paragraph (*b*)(i) or (ii) of this sub-paragraph, he was unlawfully at large or absent without leave and for that reason liable to be arrested or taken into custody ;

(*d*) any period when, his actual detention under any such power as is mentioned in paragraph (*b*)(iii) of this sub-paragraph being required or specifically authorised, he was unlawfully at large and for that reason liable to be arrested.

Interpretation

10. In this Schedule " the relevant territory " has the meaning given by section 18(3).

PRIORITY

HANDLING OF REQUESTS FOR PRIORITY TREATMENT OF CITIZENSHIP APPLICATIONS

1. Applications for registration

1.1 In most cases, consideration of applications for registration is started soon after receipt in the Nationality Directorate, and it will not normally be necessary to give an application further priority. However, where a request is made, and the reasons given satisfy the criteria in paragraph 3 below, it should be dealt with accordingly.

1.2 Where the priority request relates to a minor registration application associated with a parent's application for naturalisation, the request should be considered as follows:

a. where the application is not dependent on the outcome of the parent's application (eg applications under **s.1 (3)**), the application may be given priority;

b. where the application is dependent on the outcome of a parent's application (eg some applications under **s.3 (1)**), the application should receive priority treatment only in exceptional circumstances.

2. Applications for naturalisation

2.1 It may be possible to give a measure of priority to naturalisation applications in the circumstances set out in paragraph 3 below. The degree of priority will depend on the nature of the case and the stage it has reached. For most, the only priority which should be given is that we agree to start enquiries on the application. Where an application is nearing completion it may be possible to complete action fairly quickly. In other cases, particularly where an interview is necessary, it may not be possible to meet a given deadline and this should be explained to the applicant. The applicant should not normally be given a specific date when the application will be completed. Any estimate given should be worded in careful terms. In appropriate cases Travel Document Section may be able to help applicants if they are unable to obtain documentation from their own authorities, **but no such undertaking should be given without first consulting TDS**.

2.2 The only applications which should be treated as "immediate" at each stage are ones where we have agreed to do our best to complete the application within a specific, usually short, time-scale.

2.3 Even then it will not normally be possible to expedite a case through all its procedures since the enquiries of the police and Security Service are outside our control.

3. Criteria for priority

3.1 In deciding whether to agree to a request for priority, caseworkers should consider:

a. whether refusal of the priority request is likely to create more work (ie in justifying the refusal) than would make the refusal worthwhile; and

b. whether the application was received more than 12 months ago.

If either a. or b. is the case, consideration should normally begin immediately.

3.2 We may, in addition, consider granting a measure of priority in circumstances where an applicant:

a. is unable to make journeys necessary for compassionate or business reasons on existing documents; or

b. is approaching his or her 18th birthday and may be unable, due to mental incapacity, to take an oath of allegiance if required to do so as an adult; or

c. is stateless; or

d. is a refugee as defined by the **1951 Convention** and **1967 Protocol Relating to the Status of Refugees**; or

e. is elderly (ie 65 or over); or

f. can show that he or she needs British citizenship for a particular job; or

g. wishes to compete in a sporting or other event in this country or to represent the United Kingdom internationally. (Confirmation should be sought that the applicant is of sufficient calibre. Such cases may well attract publicity and should be seen by SEO); or

h. is the spouse of a diplomat posted, or soon to be posted, abroad (see **Chapter 18** Annex C, paragraph 6); or

i. has already been significantly inconvenienced as a result of inefficiency on the part of the Home Office. (In such cases priority should be given when the fact comes to light, regardless of whether it is requested); or

j. has secured the agreement of a minister or senior official to priority consideration; or

k. has been invited to make a fresh application (where the decision to refuse a previous application might have been made sooner but for an oversight in ND), and the new application has been received within a reasonable time after our refusal letter; or

l. has demonstrated that it would be in the national interest to consider an application out of turn despite the circumstances being otherwise undeserving.

3.3 Priority may be agreed or refused at EO level, but team leaders should be consulted if in doubt. If it is decided to give priority consideration, the EO concerned should then take responsibility for the case. Evidence justifying priority consideration may be called for at the caseworker's discretion and subject to the proviso that, as far as possible, we avoid becoming involved in protracted correspondence about whether an application does, or does not, merit priority.

4. Requests for priority in advance of an application

4.1 In certain cases, it may be decided that an application, made at some time in the future, should be granted a degree of priority. In such cases, the applicant should be notified of that decision in writing and advised, when submitting his or her application, to enclose a copy of that letter.

5. Enquiries with the police, NIS or Security Service

5.1 The police may be requested to give priority treatment to an interview (authorised at SEO level) if the case falls within the criteria in paragraph 3 above, and there are sufficiently exceptional or compassionate circumstances to justify interviewing the applicant out of turn. We should not tell applicants to contact the police.

5.2 Priority AC2/CQ checks should only be made if the case meets the criteria in paragraph 3 above, and then on the authority of an HEO (immediate) or SEO (urgent telephone check) following the procedure explained in the entry **"AC2/CQ FORMS"**.

6. Priority flags

6.1 A priority flag is marked "PRIORITY - ACTION REQUIRED BY ..... (time) .... ON .... (date)". Priority is thus set by the sending officer, and the time and date by which a response is expected will be clear. If for any reason the officer receiving the file cannot meet the deadline he or she should notify the sender as soon as possible. The priority flag should be used only when it is genuinely necessary, and sending officers should exercise discretion in setting

ANNEX E

CHAPTER 10

ENCOURAGING

CITIZENSHIP

10.1 In the UK "citizenship" normally means more than just the nationality of our inhabitants. It also encompasses elements of involvement and participation, and sharing of rights and responsibilities. Not all rights are dependent upon a person acquiring British nationality. Civil rights belong to all inhabitants, whilst political rights are enjoyed by British and Commonwealth citizens and, in some instances, EU citizens. However, the acquisition of the nationality of the country in which immigrants are living is a mark of their integration into British society. Our nationality legislation seeks to ease immigrants into acquiring citizenship by not placing unnecessary obstacles in their way. Applicants are not required to renounce the citizenship which they already hold in order to become British. Nor are British citizens required to give up their British nationality when acquiring the nationality of another State. By accepting the concept of dual citizenship, which we have done since 1948, we recognise that in the modern world, as well as owing an allegiance to the country in which they live, people also retain an affinity to the country of their roots. It is therefore possible to be a citizen of two countries and a good citizen of both.

10.2 Although we avoid placing unnecessary obstacles in the way of permanent residents who wish to acquire British citizenship, we do little positive to encourage such people to become British. The Government believes that more should be done to promote citizenship positively amongst the immigrant population, reflecting the multi-cultural and multi-racial society which we have become. However, people applying for citizenship currently have to wait too long for a decision. Quicker processing of applications would give a more welcoming signal to prospective citizens.

Nationality applications

10.3 In 1987, when the transitional provisions of the British Nationality Act 1981 came to an end, the Home Office received nearly 300,000 applications for British citizenship and average waiting times for processing these applications rose to a height of 36 months in March and April 1992. Waiting times then started to reduce, reaching 13 months in March 1995. However, since then they have started to rise gradually so that they are on average around 18 months at the present time. As mentioned in Chapter 7, nationality casework is included in the IND Casework Programme and will form part of the Integrated Casework Directorate. The efficiency improvements this will introduce will help to reduce again the processing times for applications, but a more fundamental difficulty is the inability to react speedily to a rise in the number of applications received, part of which is due to the way in which fee receipts are treated.

10.4 Applicants for British citizenship by naturalisation or registration pay a fee on application which ranges from £120 to £150. In past years, the numbers of applications received have outstripped the capacity of IND to deal with them and there is a large backlog – currently 96,000 cases are uncompleted. Intake is forecast to continue rising (from 59,600 in 1996/97 to 65,000 in 1997/98 and 70,000 in 1998/99). Waiting times will thus increase further despite process changes designed to reduce them. In view of the fee levels paid, this is impossible to defend. It is also inconsistent with our commitment to faster decisions.

Funding

10.5   Waiting times can only be reduced by applying more resources to nationality work and the Government intends to do this. As part of this strategy, consideration will be given to devising financial mechanisms which would allow the fees received from applicants in future to be better related to the resources allocated to processing citizenship cases. Together with the efficiency improvements mentioned above, this will mean that applicants will receive a better service than now.

Openness

10.6   On 22 December 1997 the Home Secretary announced that, notwithstanding section 44(2) of the British Nationality Act 1981, in future reasons would be given for refusing applications for British citizenship. Rather than operate a discretionary system in which some unsuccessful applicants were unaware why their applications had been refused or what they needed to do to make a successful application, there is now a more objective system wherein executive decisions have to be justified. That is a positive move. The Government has also set up a User Panel with representatives of applicants for citizenship in order to improve the quality of service which we offer applicants by listening to the concerns of their representatives and discussing our procedures with them.

Residence requirements

10.7   Changes in the operation of the immigration control, in particular to introduce greater flexibility in the form and manner in which leave to enter is granted, may require changes in current residence requirements for citizenship under the British Nationality Act 1981. In addition, many of those who at present cannot satisfy the requirements are those who travel abroad on behalf of firms in this country to drum up business, and thereby contribute to the economic well-being of the country and help create jobs. The Government intends to create a more flexible approach to the residence requirements based upon whether an individual was ordinarily resident in the UK and paying his or her taxes here, the overall length of their residence and connections with this country, and the reasons for their absences.

ANNEX F

Mr D McQueen
B4 Division
Lunar House

25 March 1991

cc Ms Wilkinson
    Mr Fries

H245869/2
H310363/2

Ms Spencer

APPLICATION FOR NATURALISATION : G.P. HINDUJA AND S.P. HINDUJA

This submission recommends that we refuse applications for
naturalisation made under section 6(1) of the British Nationality
Act 1981 by G.P. Hinduja and his brother S.P. Hinduja, both
citizens of India.

2.   G.P. Hinduja's application must be refused because he does
not meet the unwaivable requirement of the British Nationality
Act 1981 to have been in the UK on the date five years before his
application was received. We do not know whether S.P. Hinduja
meets that requirement as he has not submitted his passport for
the relevant period.   But from the list of absences he has
supplied it is clear that he has been out of the UK for more than
three years in the five year qualifying period. The 1981 Act
allows absences of 450 days and there is some discretion to
acquire absences in excess of this. However Ministers have never
yet agreed to waive absences on this scale. In addition, there
must be some doubt in both cases, as to whether they can be said
to meet the 1981 Act requirement to be of "good character".

BACKGROUND

3.   S.P. Hinduja was born in India in 1935 and his brother in
1940. They are internationally renowned businessmen. With two
other brothers they run Sangam Ltd and their own charitable
institution the Hinduja Foundation.   They were extremely
successful businessmen in Iran at the time of the Shah but
because of their close connections with him fled Iran at the time
of his downfall, S.P. Hinduja coming to the United Kingdom in
1981 as the sole representative of Aasia Company and G.P. Hinduja
in 1982 as the sole representative of Metralco.   In these
capacities S.P. Hinduja was given indefinite leave to remain in
this country on 18 July 1985 and G.P. Hinduja on 10 September
1986.

4. The family's business empire has a corporate wealth of between 6 and 8 billion US dollars and their personal wealth is estimated at £500 million. The Inland Revenue are currently investigating their affairs and they have told the Inland Revenue that they are not domiciled here. Domicile generally indicates the place where a person has his permanent home and we are usually slow to accept that a person whose domicile is outside the UK meets the requirement to intend, if naturalised, to make his home or principal home here.

5. The Hindujas have been pressing for their applications to be dealt with quickly because they are under investigation by the Indian authorities concerning the payment of excessive commissions on a large contract for artillery let by the previous Indian Government to the Swedish firm Bofors. This case is a major scandal in India, and contributed substantially to Gandhi's losing the election in autumn 1989. The Indian Central Bureau of Investigation filed a "first information report" on the case on 22 January 1990 naming G.P. Hinduja amongst others. This is not a charge, but a formal announcement that the person named is under investigation regarding possible offences under the Indian penal code. G.P. Hinduja has denied any involvement in the case. However, he has told officials in the FCO that he thinks it would avoid embarrassment if British citizenship were granted to him early, before the investigative process reached a more sensitive stage. The brothers may fear that the Indian Government will not renew their passports.

6. We have had to advise Ministers against accepting invitations from the brothers, (both Mrs Thatcher and Mr Waddington, when Home Secretary, were invited to attend the Diwali reception, in September 1990, which the brothers traditionally host). The FCO have asked us to avoid any appearance of special treatment in the handling of these applications. It seems that the Indian Government have in the past been quick to suspect HMG of trying to thwart it, and special treatment for the Hindujas would bring back all the old suspicions. When their naturalisation applications were received Mr Waddington asked for them to be treated in the normal way.

CONCLUSION & RECOMMENDATION

7. In view of the Bofors allegations it could be difficult for the Home Secretary to say, if challenged, that he was confident that the Hinduja brothers met the 1981 Act requirement to be of "good character". This is not defined but we do not usually grant citizenship to people who are known to be the subject of criminal investigation. Nor does it seem likely that the brothers have genuinely thrown in their lot with the UK.

8. G.P. Hinduja's application must be refused on the technical grounds of his absence from the UK on the qualifying date and we would recommend that S.P Hinduja's application also be refused on the grounds that his absences from the UK in the qualifying period are excessive. If Ministers agree with the FCO advice to treat these applications entirely on their merits, without any special treatment, we would propose to write to them advising them that their applications fall to be refused because they do

90

not meet the residence requirements of the 1981 Act and that they would be best advised to defer a further application until they are more clearly able to meet all the requirements of the British Nationality Act 1981.

9.   Mr Lloyd is invited to agree that we should refuse these applications and write on the lines suggested in paragraph 8?

D McQueen

E.R.

(45)

cc   Miss Wilkinson
      Mr Fries

Mr McQueen
B4 Division

**APPLICATION FOR NATURALISATION : G P HINDUJA
AND S P HINDUJA**

Mr Lloyd and the Home Secretary have seen
your submission of 25 March and are content
for these applications to be refused.

DIGBY GRIFFITH
Assistant Private Secretary

Private Office
3 April 1991

ANNEX G

From : A Walmsley   cc   Home Secretary
       Nationality Directorate   Ms Quin
       India Buildings   Permanent Secretary
                                           Mr Walker
       3 July 1997   Mr Rawsthorne
                                           Mr Warner
                                           Mr Owen

Mr O'Brien

APPLICATION FOR NATURALISATION - MR G P HINDUJA (H245869)

Issue to be decided

1.   Whether to grant the application for naturalisation made by
Mr G P Hinduja.

Timing

2.   Routine, although the matter has been raised with you orally
by Mr Keith Vaz, and one of Mr Hinduja's referees, Lord Feldman,
is also pressing for an early decision.

Summary

3.   Mr G P Hinduja applied for naturalisation in March 1997
after an earlier application made in April 1990 was refused in
April 1991 because of his failure to meet the unwaivable
residence requirement of being in the United Kingdom on the date
5 years before his application was made.

Recommendation

4.   That the application be granted.

Consideration

5.   Mr G P Hinduja was born in India in 1940.   He is an
internationally renowned businessman and, with his elder brother
Mr S P Hinduja and two other brothers not apparently living in
the United Kingdom, runs Sangam Ltd and their own charitable
institution, the Hinduja Foundation.   They were extremely
successful businessmen in Iran at the time of the Shah but fled
at the time of his downfall because of their close connection
with him. Mr G P Hinduja was granted indefinite leave to remain
in the United Kingdom on 10 September 1986.   The family's
business empire has a corporate wealth between 6 and 8 billion
US dollars and their personal wealth was estimated in 1991 at
being £500 million.

6.   When he applied for naturalisation in 1990 Mr G P Hinduja's
application was refused because he failed to meet the requirement
to have been in the United Kingdom on the date 5 years' previous
to his application being received. (This date starts the
qualifying period of 5 years in which absences from the United
Kingdom count against the normal limit of 450 days in the
period.)   On this occasion, Mr Hinduja was in the UK on the

requisite date in 1992 but he has been absent from the United Kingdom for 540 days against the normal permitted level of 450 set out in Schedule 1 to the British Nationality Act 1981. However, there is discretion to waive absences in excess of the 450 limit if in the special circumstances of a particular case it seems right to do so. In deciding whether or not to exercise discretion in favour of an applicant who fails to meet this requirement, we would normally take into account the total length of residence in the UK, whether an applicant has established his home and family here, whether he has transferred the bulk of his estate to the United Kingdom and the reasons for his absences. In Mr Hinduja's case he has been resident here for 15 years, his wife and adult children live here (and are applying for citizenship separately), Sangam Ltd is established in the UK although India remains the centre of their business empire, and Mr Hinduja's absences have been caused primarily by business trips abroad. In these circumstances I would recommend that the excess absences be waived. It would be fully in accordance with current practice to do so.

6. At the time of his earlier application there were also doubts, not disclosed to the applicant about whether Mr G P Hinduja could meet the requirement to be "of good character". The Inland Revenue were said to have been investigating the Hinduja's affairs and the Indian authorities were said to be investigating the payment of excessive commissions on a large contract for artillery let by the previous Indian Government of Mr Rajiv Gandhi to the Swedish firm Bofors. This was a major scandal in India at the time and Mr G P Hinduja was named, amongst others, as being under investigation.

7. In connection with the current application a letter has been produced from Mr Hinduja's Inspector of Taxes confirming that they are satisfied that his tax affairs are in order and up to date. (It is our normal practice to require such letters from businessmen and self-employed persons, especially where there are excess absences.) We have also consulted the Foreign and Commonwealth Office about the application. Their view is that whilst the Bofors affair is not a dead issue interest in it has lessened and it is unlikely that the Indian authorities would be concerned one way or the other about the outcome of Mr Hinduja's application for naturalisation. After such a length of time without any proceedings being initiated against Mr Hinduja it would not seem right to continue to harbour doubts about his ability to meet the "good character" requirement. I would recommend that the application be granted.

Handling

8. There are no handling/presentational issues. India is a country which does not allow dual citizenship so Mr Hinduja is unlikely to publicise his acquisition of British citizenship because by doing so he would forfeit Indian citizenship and, possibly, the right to own property in India.

A WALMSLEY

ANNEX H

RESTRICTED

Foreign &
Commonwealth
Office

London SW1A 2AH

Telephone: 0171

08 November 1996

Andrew Walmsley
Director
Nationality Division
IND
Home Office
3rd Floor India Buildings
Water Street, LIVERPOOL L2 0QN

Dear Mr. Walmsley,

THE HINDUJA BROTHERS

1. Thank you for your letter of 5 November.

2. The Hinduja family are certainly controversial figures.
They are immensely wealthy, influential (with close political
contacts in India with the Congress and Bharatiya Janata
Parties) and secretive. The Hinduja trading empire (valued at
over £1.5 billion) was started by their late father in Bombay,
and later prospered in Iran under the Shah. Rumours abound
that the Hindujas made a lot of money at this time through
arms dealing - though the Hindujas have always vehemently
denied this. Business associates of theirs include Adnan
Kashoggi and Chandraswami (now under arrest in India on
cheating charges).

3. As you know, G P and S P Hinduja have been based in London
since 1981, with another brother (Prakash) in Geneva and a
fourth (Ashok) in Bombay. Their worldwide activities now
include banking, investment finance, trade and marketing,
manufacturing (they acquired the Indian bus and truck maker
Ashok Leyland in 1987), oil (they control the Gulf Oil Trading
Company), power (in a project with National Power),
construction (linked to Bechtel, the US company), aviation,
the media and the film industry.

4. Controversy dogged the Hinduja family in the 1980s. After
years of rumours concerning their role in corrupt payments in
the Bofors arms deal signed by the Rajiv Gandhi Government GP
was named in a criminal investigation pursued by the

RESTRICTED

shortlived (1989-90) Janata Dal government. Three Swiss bank accounts, allegedly linked to GP, were frozen. Although GP has repeatedly and strenuously denied the allegations, the rumours still surface periodically and pressure from certain quarters to get access to the accounts continues today. According to the Indian media, the Swiss banks have recently released relevant documents. Given the activism of the Indian courts, it is conceivable that the case could come alight.

5.   At the very least the Hinduja brothers can be said to have sailed close to the wind in building their business empire. Beyond that nothing has, to our knowledge, been proved. They certainly have enemies, including in the media, elements of which have sought to keep alive the controversy surrounding the family. As a result we believe there is bound to be some Indian Government nervousness about its close involvement in projects which the Hindujas are funding or in which they are heavily involved. Hence the advice in Sam Sharpe's letter of 7 October to Edward Oakden about the celebrations of India's 50th anniversary of Independence (not of partition). We do not, however, believe that the Indian Government would be particularly concerned by a decision either to grant or refuse GP Hinduja British nationality.

6. You may wish to seek the DTI's views on the Hindujas' business practices in the UK.

Caroline Elmes
South Asian Department

ANNEX I

From: Matthew LAXTON
To: INDINDIA.B4(AWALMSLEY)
Date: Thursday, 2 July 1998 11:20 am
Subject: J P HINDUJA (H300363)

You will be aware that Mr O'Brien is keen to adopt a more
positive approach
to citizenship. In your submission of 27 February on the same
subject, one
of the areas that you mentioned was where people had their
applications
refused on the grounds of excessive absences. Mr O'Brien has
recently had
brought to his attention the case of Mr Hinduja whose application
was
refused in 1991 for that reason.

On the sketchy details that have been provided, it would appear
that Mr H
is a businessman/entrepreneur who runs a group of companies. He
still
spends a lot of time out of the country (190 days in 1993, 200
in 1994,
 163 in 1995, 155 in 1996 and 111 in 1997) but believes that it
is
justified because his work benefits the country. The Minister
would like to
know:

i) Is it correct that Mr H was refused for the reason given?

ii) Has the policy changed in this area since 1991?

iii) Would Mr H be likely to benefit from a positive approach to
citizenship? (as far as I know, Mr H does not have an
outstanding
application)

Thank you for your assistance.

ANNEX J

BACKGROUND NOTE

Mr Baker's Question follows on from an earlier Question dated 24 November 2000, a copy of which is attached.

There have been no direct representations concerning these applications from the Rt Hon Member for Hartlepool (Mr Mandelson). I understand that Mr Mandelson did speak to Mr O'Brien in 1998 about the general circumstances surrounding the refusal of Mr S P Hinduja's application and the likelihood of him benefiting from the Government's positive attitude to citizenship, particularly regarding the residence requirements. A copy of the enquiry is attached but I do not have a copy of my response. I do not consider this enquiry to be representations on the application. *Now available*

In October 1998 I received a telephone call from Mr Vaz about the progress on Mr S P Hinduja's application. At the time no application had been received and I was arranging for Mr Hinduja to re-sign and re-date his original application form (which he did on 20 October 1998).

A copy of Mr Vaz's subsequent letter to me is attached. Again, I would not consider these to be representations about the application, more of a progress enquiry. *Now attached*

From :Mike O'Brien   cc. Home Secretary

ANNEX K

20 December 2000

Barbara Roche

HINDUJA BROTHERS

1. My concern with regard to the PQ is that the wording in the suggested answer is ambiguous on the denial of 'representations' and ought to be clearer. Representations can mean a request for information or a letter of support.

2. Keith Vaz and Peter Mandelson made enquiries. I understand Keith Vaz enquired in 1997 about when a decision could be expected in the cases. Peter Mandelson requested information on how an application might be viewed under the Home Office policy of encouraging citizenship, but as far as I recall, did not make representations asking that an application be granted.

3. In both Hinduja cases officials recommended that the applications be accepted.

MIKE O'BRIEN

From: Alan Underwood   cc: Home Secretary
        Director   Ministers
        ICD North   Hilary Jackson
        3rd Floor   Mara Goldstein
        India Buildings   Cathy Hume
                                             David Barnes
                                             John Warne
                                             Stephen Boys Smith
                                             Chris Mace
                                             Farida Eden
                                             Harry Carter
Date   23 January 2001   Chris Hudson
                                             Brian Caffarey
                                             Anna Michael (Parly Section)
                                             Alan Gibson (Ppt Agency)
                                             Gillian Kirton
                                             Chris Kelly
                                             Gemma Smith
                                             Rosemary Earp
                                             Deidre Wright

Pam Teare

HINDUJA : LINES TO TAKE

There have been numerous developments on this matter since my note of
yesterday to Gemma Smith, not copied to all those above.

2.   This note summarises those developments and also provides a strong
health warning on the disclosure of names listed in my earlier note as having an
interest in the naturalisation applications of SP and GP Hinduja.   A separate
note went out earlier this morning to recipients of the first note. Legal advice
on this point had been that provided individuals have already been named
publicly, eg in PQs or in the newspapers, we too can refer to them by name.
The names must be in the public domain; otherwise we need their consent.

Latest procedural advice suggests, however, that the specific wording of recent PQs means that we should respond only on enquiries made to the current Secretary of State.

3.   Media enquiries have mainly focussed on the reply to Norman Baker's recent PQ (copy attached at Annex A) asking what representations had been received on behalf of SP and GP Hinduja from Keith Vaz and Peter Mandelson. Pam Teare is currently working on the detailed response on this aspect.

4.   Conscious of the fact that the John Cryer PQ (Annex B) will raise additional questions around this topic I attach revised background briefing and Q&A for Press Office and others' use (Annex C). Further named day PQs have also just been received from Norman Baker on the same subject and will require a co-ordinated response, considered across Private Offices, Press Office and the ICD.

ALAN UNDERWOOD

ANNEX M

Norman Baker: To ask the Secretary of State for the Home Department what representations he has received on the applications by GP Hindiya and SP Hindiya for British citizenship from (a) the Right honourable member for Hartlepool and (b) the honourable Member for Leicester East.

DRAFT REPLY (BARBARA ROCHE)

I presume the Hon Member is referring to the applications for naturalisation made by Mr G P Hinduja and Mr S P Hinduja.

Two Members made enquiries about the cases. The Honourable Member for Leicester East about when a decision could be expected in the cases, and the Rt Honourable Member for Hartlepool about how an application might be viewed given the Government's wider policy of encouraging citizenship from long-standing residents who fulfilled the criteria.

[handwritten note: Sarah find out what/how Jack. When I raised this with I can't remember.]

ANNEX N

Secretary of State

NORMAN BAKER PQ: HINDUJA BROTHERS

You will recall the Norman Baker Question about the Hinduja brothers.

I have spoken with the Home Secretary's vate Office and with Mike O'Brien's office.

I'm told you raised the issue with Mike C   en, either in a telephone call or a personal note. Mike O'Brien does not re   ber how precisely you raised it but he does remember you asked how an applic   n for citizenship by the Hinduja brothers might be viewed given the posit   contribution their work makes to the country.

As your exchange with Mike O'Brien wa   ring the time you were Minister without Portfolio, the only record that exists is th   tached copy of an e-mail from Matthew Laxton (Mike O'Brien's Private Secretary   an official in the Home Office. The e-mail was in response to your query th   it makes no reference to you by name.

The Question is overdue for answer and   Home Office are keen to reply to it as soon as possible – see the attached sligh   amended Answer.

As a matter of interest, several Oppositi   MPs also made representations/ supported the Hinduja brothers' citizen   , so if there is a partisan reaction to the Answer, the plan would be to bring this

Are you content for the Answer to be pt   wn as drafted?

Sarah Todd

SARAH
11 January 2001

/LMcC

OBSERVER
21/01/01

Mandelson helped Dome backer's passport bid

by Antony Barnett, Gaby Hinsliff and Luke Harding Delhi

PETER MANDELSON helped a controversial Indian tycoon, who is currently facing corruption charges, to obtain British citizenship after he and his brother agreed to donate £1 million to bail out the Millennium Dome.

In what was last night being called a 'passports-for-favours' scandal, *The Observer* can reveal that Mandelson approached the Home Office to find out whether an application from Srichand Hinduja, who had already been turned down for a British passport, would be welcomed.

Hinduja duly applied in March 1999 and received his passport six months later – a third of the time a typical decision takes.

Calling for an urgent investigation, Liberal Democrat MP Norman Baker said last night: 'We have a rich businessman in the middle of a corruption scandal who gets a British passport in record time after donating £1m to the Dome. It now appears the Minister responsible for the

Dome helped to get him a passport. We need a clear statement on who lobbied the Home Office on the Hindujas' behalf and when.'

Alison Stanley, a senior immigration lawyer with the legal firm Bindmans and head of the Law Society's immigration panel, said: 'It appears highly unusual. The only time the Home Office fast-tracks a court investigating corruption charges, but they were refused permission to leave the country. Federal Indian police allege that the brothers sought British citizenship to frustrate any attempts to extradite. Gopichand was granted British citizenship in November 1997.

The two have networked citizenship is if there are exceptional circumstances such as a parent without a passport who needs to visit a seriously ill child overseas.'

Mandelson, the Northern Ireland Secretary, last night issued a statement insisting his involvement had been only in finding out the lay of the land and denied he had lobbied for Hinduja to get a passport. 'To the limited extent that I was involved in this matter I was always very sensitive to the proprieties,' he said. 'The matter was dealt with by my private secretary. At no time did I support or endorse this application for citizenship.'

Two days ago, Srichand and his brother Gopichand were granted bail by an Indian

their way to the heart of the British Establishment, inviting Tony and Cherie Blair as guests of honour to a lavish party celebrating Diwali. Four days after Srichand got his passport, they hosted a reception at their London offices in honour of the British legal system to which Mandelson was invited.

Mandelson was also a frequent visitor to their central London offices when he was a Minister without Portfolio and Trade Secretary, and one source recalls a dinner Blair and Mandelson had at the Hindujas' central London home before the election.

But their real entrée into New Labour society came through the Dome. Mandelson was Minister in charge of it when the Hindujas offered £1m to fund its faith zone. The brothers are understood to have approached Mandelson after the deal was concluded, asking him to find out how an application by Srichand would be received by the Government. He asked his private secretary at the Cabinet Office to make inquiries of the Immigration Minister.

The disclosure of Mandelson's role will raise questions about the relationship between New Labour and its rich business friends. *The Observer* can reveal that Keith Vaz, now Minister for Europe, also approached the Home Office to ask when a decision would be made in the case of Gopichand. Vaz refused to comment on his involvement in the affair.

Sources close to Mandelson insisted the approach came only after the negotiations over the brothers' involvement in the Dome were finished.

His account also clashes with that of Home Office officials who said Mandelson made representations in mid-1997, when negotiations over the Dome were likely to have been taking place.

RESTRICTED AND PERSONAL

ANNEX P

Secretary of the Cabinet and Head of the Home Civil Servi

JONATHAN POWELL   cc   Robin Young
                                                  Joe Pilling
                                                  John Warne
                                                  Clare Sumner

HINDUJAS AND PETER MANDELSON

You asked me for advice about Peter Mandelson and the Hindujas.

Principles

2.   The following seem to be the main points of principle:

  i.   it must be primarily for Peter Mandelson to explain and defend
          what happened between him and the Hindujas on the passport
          application. The only issue for the Prime Minister is whether
          anything that has happened causes him to lose confidence in
          Peter Mandelson;

  ii.   there is nothing wrong in a Minister who has been lobbied about a
          passport application passing it on to the Home Office, adding a
          comment on the merits of the application if he wishes. This
          happens under all Governments;

  iii.   it would be on the wrong side of the line if a Minister were to press
          the Home Office to grant a passport application in return for the
          individual concerned doing a favour, either for the Government (eg
          investing in the Dome) or personally. There are obvious
          gradations of behaviour here. Support for an application at a time
          when the Minister is coincidentally having dealings on another
          matter with the individual making the application is a slippery
          area and would need to be handled with care to avoid
          misinterpretation;

  iv.   it would be seriously wrong, and open to judicial review, if the
          Home Office Minister making the decision on the proposed
          application were to do so on the strength of some irrelevant and
          extraneous factor (eg whether the individual had contributed to
          the Dome).

RESTRICTED AND PERSONAL

RESTRICTED AND PERSONAL

Applying the Principles to this Case

3.   Getting at the facts on the Hindujas' application has not been easy but this is the story as I understand it.

4.   Both S P and G P Hinduja applied for naturalisation in 1990 and had their applications refused in 1991. In February 1998 Mr S Hinduja wrote to Mr Mandelson offering to underwrite the Spirit Zone at the Dome to the tune of £3m and Mr Mandelson got to know him as a result of this offer of sponsorship. I understand that Mr S Hinduja believed that as a result of a change in the law it might be worth making a fresh application but he did not want to apply if he would be refused automatically as a result of the earlier decision. He mentioned this to Peter Mandelson. In June 1998 Peter Mandelson had a short telephone conversation with Mike O'Brien and established that a fresh application by Mr Hinduja would be considered on its merits according to the criteria then applying and without reference to the earlier decision.   A trawl of the Home Office files has revealed no correspondence between Mr Mandelson and the Home Office about S P or G P Hinduja.

5.   We have said publicly that Peter Mandelson is still clear that he did not sponsor or endorse the application or make representations on Mr S Hinduja's behalf.   The Home Office have confirmed this.   Barbara Roche answered a Written PQ on 18 January about the applications for naturalisation made by G P Hinduja and S P Hinduja. The answer said that Peter Mandelson 'made inquiries about how an application might be viewed given the Government's wider policy of encouraging citizenship from long-standing residents who fulfilled the criteria, but did not make representations that an application be granted.'

6.   There was an unfortunate minor mix-up about who spoke to the Home Office. The line taken at the lobby on 22 January was that Mr Mandelson had had asked his private secretary to refer the issue to the Home Office. Chris Smith said in the House that Mr Mandelson's Parliamentary Private Secretary had been involved. On further reflection, Mr Mandelson recalled that he had spoken to Mike O'Brien personally rather than his private secretary speaking to Mike O'Brien's office. Alastair Campbell ironed this wrinkle out at this morning's lobby. Chris Smith will also issue a correction.

7.   One final part of the story. While Secretary of State for Northern Ireland, Mr Mandelson received a letter in May 2000 from G P Hinduja about a possible citizenship application from a third brother, Prakash, whom Mr Mandelson has never met.   Mr Mandelson gave the letter to the Home Secretary without support or endorsement. The Home Secretary wrote to Mr Mandelson in June 2000 explaining the procedures for naturalisation

RESTRICTED AND PERSONAL

RESTRICTED AND PERSONAL

applications. The Hindujas sent Peter Mandelson some mangoes around the same time. There has been no application from Prakash. This part of the story (less the mangoes) was announced at this morning's lobby.

Conclusion

8.   My best guess is that this case falls into the slippery area where a Minister, having official dealings with someone, coincidentally and separately passes on a question about an application for a passport from that person to the Home Office. This is what Mr Mandelson would appear to have done both with the letter about Prakash and in the case of S P Hinduja. The best course in such cases is to stand back from the application and make it clear that the Minister is simply forwarding orally or in writing the question about whether it would be worth applying (S P Hinduja) or a letter about a possible application (Prakash). The more strongly the Minister supports the application, the more awkward the perception. But at the end of the day the decision about an application is for the Home Office and as a matter of integrity they would not be influenced by irrelevant considerations, whatever their source. Home Office Ministers and Mr Mandelson have made clear their view that he did nothing improper in either case.

9.   I suggest that the Prime Minister and Number 10 should not get too involved in this. The line should simply be:

    i.   where a Minister is approached about a passport application there is nothing wrong in his passing on the information to the Home Office, adding a comment if he wishes;

    ii.   all that happened here was that Peter Mandelson made a phone call to a Home Office Minister and established that a fresh application from Mr S Hinduja would be considered on its merits according to the criteria then applying and without reference to the decision in 1991 to refuse his earlier application; and pass on to the Home Office a letter about Prakash. He did not support either application or make representations;

    iii. no one has produced a shred of evidence that anything improper took place.

Richard Wilson
pp **RICHARD WILSON**

23 January 2001

RESTRICTED AND PERSONAL

ANNEX Q

From :   Andrew Walmsley
           Nationality Directorate
           India Buildings

           14 August 1998

Mr O'Brien

MR S P HINDUJA (H300363)

Issue to be decided

1.   You asked for advise on whether Mr Hinduja would benefit
from any change of policy regarding excess absences for people
applying for naturalisation.

Timing

2.   Now pressing as I believe you would like to clear the matter
before you go on holiday.

Summary

3.   Mr Srichand Hinduja applied for naturalisation in April 1990
along with his brother Gopichand.   Both applications were
refused: in Gopichand's case it was because he was unable to meet
the unwaivable requirement to have been in the UK on the date 5
years before his application was received.   Srichand's
application was refused because he had been out of the UK for
1233 days out of a possible 1825 days in the 5 year period.
Since the applications were refused in April 1991 Gopichand
re-applied for naturalisation in March 1997 and his application
was granted, after reference to you, in November 1997. He had
been out of the UK for 540 days, compared with the normal 450
days, but Srichand has apparently been absent for 819 days in the
5 years 1993-1997. We have no indication how many days he has
been absent in 1998.

Recommendation

4.   That you indicate to Mr Hinduja that we would be inclined
to look favourably on his application provided he is resident in
the UK for tax purposes, and suggest that his solicitor gets in
touch with me.

Consideration

5.   Along with his brother, Gopichand, and two other brothers
not apparently living in the UK, Mr Hinduja runs Sangam Ltd and
the family's own charitable institution, the Hinduja Foundation.
The family's business empire has a corporate wealth of between
6 and 8 billion US dollars and their personal wealth was
estimated in 1991 at £500 million.

6. At the time of his earlier application Mr Hinduja was absent for most of the 5 years prior to his application. He would seem to have reduced the level of his absences and, although they are high at 819, they are within the upper limit of what we would consider waiving. In deciding whether or not to exercise discretion in favour of an applicant who fails to meet this residence requirement, we would normally take into account the total length of residence in the UK, whether an applicant has established his home and family here, whether he has transferred the bulk of his estate here, and the reasons for his absence. Sangam Ltd is established in the UK although India remains the centre of the family's business empire, Mr Hinduja's family are here with him and his absences have no doubt been caused by business trips abroad.

7. At the time of his earlier application there were doubts about the brothers' ability to meet the requirement to be of "good character. These centred on a reported Inland Revenue investigation of their tax affairs and their alleged part in the Bofors scandal in India which concerned excessive commissions paid to the Indian Government of Mr Gandhi by the Swedish firm. These were, however, resolved concerning Mr Gopichand Hinduja's application and there is no reason to believe that Mr Srichand Hinduja would not now meet the requirement.

Handling/presentational issues

8. None.

A WALMSLEY

ANNEX R

PARLIAMENTARY UNDER
SECRETARY OF STATE

HOME OFFICE
QUEEN ANNE'S GATE
LONDON SW1H 9AT

Peter Mandelson Esq MP
House of Commons
LONDON
SW1A 0AA

r ref: IMP H300363

5 OCT 1998

Dear Peter

You may recall that you were in contact with my office last month concerning Mr
S P Hinduja who is considering submitting an application to naturalise as a British
citizen. I am sorry that I have not responded sooner.

I am sure that you will appreciate that without a formal application, I cannot give
you a definitive answer as to whether any application that Mr Hinduja may choose
to make would be successful. However, my officials advise me that his current
level of absences from the United Kingdom are not considered excessive and that
they are likely to look favourably upon any application. The Director of the
Nationality Directorate in Liverpool, Andrew Walmsley, has told me that he is
always happy to advise future applicants on their chances of success and Mr
Hinduja's representatives may wish to consider contacting him. His address is: -
Nationality Directorate, 3rd Floor, India Buildings, Water Street, Liverpool L2
0QN.

I hope that this information is useful.

Yours
Mike

MIKE O'BRIEN

ANNEX S

Gopichand P. Hinduja

GPH/ME

18 May, 2000

The Rt Hon Peter Mandelson, MP
Secretary of State for Northern Ireland
The Northern Ireland Office
LONDON SW1

PRIVATE AND CONFIDENTIAL

Dear Peter,

It has been a long time since we last met, but I am following the progress in Northern Ireland with great interest. I hope you are keeping well.

I know you are very busy and I am sorry to be troubling you. But I need your help and advice.

You will recall that last year my brother S P was also granted British Citizenship in view of his lengthy residence in Britain and now our entire family have become British Citizens and we have made London our home.

Now our brother Prakash who is a resident of Switzerland, but also spends part of his time in UK as he is the Director and majority shareholder of our UK based company, Sangam Ltd would also like to take up British Citizenship.

As we see it, there are two major hurdles regarding his application

1 – He needs to become a permanent resident of UK
2 – Meet the residents' requirement of spending only 450 days in 5 years outside UK

However, on the plus side, the benefits he would bring as a UK Citizen would far out weigh any hurdles that there may be. By becoming a British Citizen and making his home in London, Prakash would orientate himself towards Britain and would bring much investment and trade particularly in the field of information technology with him.

Cont.../2

For UK correspondence
New Zealand House, 14th Floor, 80 Haymarket, London SW1Y 4TE
Telephone: 0171 839 4661 Fax: 0171 839 5990

-2-

The Rt Hon Peter Mandelson, MP   18 May, 2000

Would it be possible for you to find out if the Home Office would consider such an application from Prakash.

S.P joins me in sending you our best wishes for your continued good health and success.

With warmest personal regards.

Yours sincerely,

Gopichand P Hinduja

ANNEX T

QUEEN ANNE'S GATE
LONDON SW1H 9AT

Personal

25 May 2000.

Dear Peter,

When we met yesterday you passed me a letter you had received from G. P. Hinduja about whether his brother/could gain British citizenship.

I'm pursuing the matter up personally & will be both in touch as soon as I can.

Yrs ever
Jack.

Rt Hon Peter Mandelson MP.

From :	Andrew Walmsley	cc	Barbara Roche
	ICD (Liverpool)		Sir David Omand
	Mercury Court		Stephen Boys Smith
			Peter Wrench
			Bob Whalley
	22 June 2000		Pam Teare
			Ed Owen
			Justin Russell

Home Secretary

PRAKASH HINDUJA – ENQUIRY FROM RT. HON. PETER MANDELSON

Issue to be decided

How to respond to the request from the Secretary of State for Northern Ireland about Mr Hinduja's wish to become a British citizen.

Timing

Routine.

Summary

Mr Prakash Hinduja wishes to become a British citizen like his two brothers, Gopichand and Srichand, and other members of his family. To do this he would need to make a successful application for naturalisation for which he would need to meet certain statutory requirements regarding residence in the United Kingdom. The most important of these, and the biggest stumbling block in the context of Mr Hinduja's application, is the requirement that he should have indefinite leave to remain in the United Kingdom under the immigration law and rules. He presently resides in Switzerland and, on the face of it, he would not be able to meet this requirement.

Recommendation

That you reply to Mr Mandelson on the lines of the attached draft.

Consideration

To qualify for naturalisation Mr Prakash Hinduja would need to have lived in the United Kingdom for 5 years with no more than 450 days' absence during this period (although there is discretion to waive excess absences in appropriate cases) and have indefinite leave to remain here under the immigration laws. He is presently residing in Switzerland and would not appear to be able to meet these requirements. To qualify for naturalisation he must first have indefinite leave to remain in the United Kingdom. He must therefore first seek to establish himself here, for which, given the family's wealth, he would no doubt qualify as an investor or a person of independent means or as a businessman

114

Mr Hinduja's two elder brothers, Gopichand and Srichand, have both been naturalised within the past three years. They too had initial difficulties over meeting the residence requirements but were able to make successful applications after we were able to offer advice through their company's legal adviser, Richard Hoare, about the timing of the applications. That would appear to be the most sensible way to proceed regarding Mr Prakash Hinduja as much would depend on his personal circumstances and the strength of his connections with the United Kingdom about which we have very little information at present.

Handling/presentational issues

The Hinduja brothers were reputed to have been involved in an arms scandal involving the Swedish arms company Bofors and members of Mr Gandhi's Indian Government at the start of the 1990s. The brothers were alleged to have acted as intermediaries between the company and Indian Ministers who received illegal payments for awarding the contract to the company. No action was ever taken against the brothers by Mr Gandhi's successors and it is doubtful after this length of time whether action ever will. The brothers are unlikely to draw attention to their acquisition of British citizenship and their brother's application because India is a single nationality country and obtaining British citizenship will have caused them to lose their Indian nationality. That in turn could affect their right to own property in India.

ANDREW WALMSLEY

ANNEX V

QUEEN ANNE'S GATE LONDON SW1H 9AT

The Rt Hon Peter Mandelson MP
House of Commons
LONDON
SW1A OAA

26 JUN 2000

Dear Peter,

PRAKASH HINDUJA

I said I would write to you again about Prakash Hinduja's interest in British citizenship.

As Gopichand Hinduja acknowledges in his letter to you of 18 May, as his brother is resident in Switzerland he would first need to settle in the United Kingdom and be granted indefinite leave to remain here before he could apply for naturalisation. This is an unwaivable requirement of the British Nationality Act. There is discretion though to waive any excess absences for an applicant, and I think the next step should be for one of my officials to speak to Richard Hoare, Mr Gopichand Hinduja's legal adviser, about Mr Prakash Hinduja. We would then be able to offer advice on how he might obtain settlement under the immigration rules and on the timing of any application for citizenship. I have therefore asked Mr Andrew Walmsley, Deputy Director of the Integrated Casework Directorate in Liverpool, Tel. 0151 237 8017 to contact Mr Hoare to discuss Mr Prakash Hinduja's situation with him.

I hope this is helpful. I'd be happy to have a further word with you.

Yours,

Jack.

JACK STRAW

2199js

Printed in the United Kingdom by The Stationery Office Limited
03/01   599762   19585

116